The Emperor's New Computer: *ICT, Teachers and Teaching*

Edited by
Tony Di Petta
Brock University, Canada

SENSE PUBLISHERS
ROTTERDAM/TAIPEI

A C.I.P. record for this book is available from the Library of Congress.

ISBN 978-90-8790-655-9 (paperback)
ISBN 978-90-8790-656-6 (hardback)
ISBN 978-90-8790-657-3 (e-book)

Published by: Sense Publishers
P.O. Box 21858, 3001 AW
Rotterdam, The Netherlands
http://www.sensepublishers.com

Printed on acid-free paper

The Emperor
ICT, Teachers and Teaching

TABLE OF CONTENTS

THE EMPEROR'S NEW COMPUTER

Introduction

The landscape of contemporary education increasingly reflects a wired and frenetic world of instantaneous communication where student *technophiles* abound adept at message transmitting and receiving using an ever-expanding array of information and communication technologies (ICT). Blackberrys, Instant Messaging, I-Pods, I-Phones, and other cell phones with gaming, multimedia, MP3, video, and e-mail capabilities are a few of the technological gadgets that a generation raised on video-games, the Internet, and relentless marketing cannot live without. For these *technokinder*, information technology is not something to be learned or feared but rather it is what they have grown up with as their playthings and within the space of a generation these so-called toys have become the essential technologies of an Internet connected, globally oriented and communication obsessed population. Interestingly, the popularity of the Internet is becoming problematic for some members of the wired generation, so much so that the American Psychological Association is considering including Internet Addiction Disorder in the Diagnostic and Statistical Manual of Mental Disorders. Moreover, social networking sites such as Youtube and MySpace, which connect more than a hundred million people, mostly under the age of 35 in a *virtual agora* for sharing ideas, videos, music, and discussion on a daily basis, are becoming powerful factors in the reinvention of everything from education to political debate. Another technokinder web destination "Second Life: or something like it" re-creates the real world as a virtual space, a brave new virtual environment where everything from business to education can be re-imagined and lived as its denizens envision. Second Life residents, currently more than a million people worldwide, spend between 10 and 20 hours a week online living their virtual lives in their mutually constructed virtual world environments.

The virtual world and the real world are starting to collide however, and the consequences are of particular interest to educators seeking to understand how the new technologies for information and communication sharing will affect and redefine teaching and learning. Some educators do not view the enticements of this new age of interconnection supported through ICT as particularly suited to traditional schooling and they suggest that these so-called "toys" are as dangerous as they are alluring. Fearing the real or imagined damage that information and communication technologies may do to education, these *technoskeptics* express doubt about the cost, complexity, over-reliance upon, and ever increasing demands for the latest thing that information and communication technologies seem to engender in education. From this perspective, the new technologies are suspect, a form of insidious gadgetry that can take over teachers professional lives and intrude into their private lives as well. Moreover, some argue that these technologies may be

T. Di Petta (Ed.), The Emperor's New Computer: ICT, Teachers and Teaching, 1–4.

alienating and isolating students from the world around them and perhaps even from themselves.

Ethical questions about what can or should be done with ICT loom large in the technoskeptic perspective, leading some to yearn nostalgically for the "Good Old Days," that mythical time when the human touch was thought to be ever present in education and machines were kept at a respectful distance, decrying the intrusive and arcane nature of the virtual world of "techies" and "cyberspace."

The landscape of information and communication technology in education presented in *The Emperor's New Computer* is not dominated by technophiles or technoskeptics however. The view reflected in the explorations of ICT and education presented here is that the vast majority of students, teachers, and other citizens of the contemporary wired world of education are best described as *technopragmatists*, who prudently ask, what lies behind the hype and fashion or what can technology do for me, and what will it cost? The Emperor's New Computer is a pragmatic re-visioning of the fable of the Emperor's New Clothes, looking behind the fashionable masks and costumes of ICT and examining how information and communication technologies affect the complex process of human interconnection known as teaching and learning.

In Chapter One, William Warren, from the University of Newcastle in Australia, examines the philosophy of technology as it has evolved from the Sophists of ancient Greece to the post-modernists of the present day. He argues for a re-engagement of the technological debate in contemporary societies where advanced technology shapes, and is shaped by, the complex activity of teaching and the role of the teacher as "reflective practitioners."

In Chapter Two, Stéphane Lévesque, from the University of Ottawa in Canada, argues that ICT in its current form cannot be integrated directly into classrooms without complicated and time-consuming educational transformations that restrict what teachers can do to help their students learn with technology. He notes that the primary features of the current technologies available to school-based users rarely match the pedagogical demands of students and teachers. Lévesque introduces a program called the Virtual Historian which he uses to discuss the implications of working with technology in the classroom and to argue for the development of technological pedagogical content knowledge as an additional knowledge base for the successful integration of technology in education.

In Chapter Three, Kevin Kee, from Brock University in Canada, explores similar technology classroom integration questions through the development of a simulation of the *Canadian War Measures Act* used during World War I, World War II, and the 1970 October Crisis in Quebec to arrest and detain innocent people. He examines how teachers in social studies and civics classes can use technological tools such as simulations to teach students about the past and to provide them with opportunities to elucidate contemporary dilemmas by situating them within an historical context.

Chapter Four by Yngve Troye Nordkvelle of Lillehammer University College, Norway and Randi Tosterud from Gjøvik University College, Norway looks behind the curtain of Learning Management Systems used throughout higher education institutes and increasingly in primary and secondary schools in Europe and North

America, and ponders the Orwellian capabilities that these management systems endow on educational administrations and administrators. The authors discuss the implications for students, teachers, and teaching that such technological surveillance might entail and explore the perceptions of students on what it means "to be and to be observed" in these online educational environments.

In Chapter Five, Ferdinand J. Potgieter, from North-West University in South Africa, argues for an African perspective on educational mobile computing (the use of handheld computers, smartphones, and other mobile technologies in education) in order to counteract the largely Western notions of individualism and technocracy that have dominated the direction and application of these technologies since their inception. He discusses the differences between Western and African perspectives on life, humanity and learning and raises critical concerns arguing for a philosophy of technology to which more people from non-western nations can subscribe.

In Chapter Six, Huang Yuxing and Tang Xiayun from Fujian Normal University in China and Li Xiaobin from Brock University, Canada explore how Chinese higher education has changed since the economic globalization promoted by China's inclusion in the World Trade Organization. The authors discuss how China's increasing use of ICT in education and in society generally might be used to promote political multi-lateralism and national multiculturalism.

In Chapter Seven, Stephen Petrina, Oksana Bartosh, Ruth Guo, and Linda Stanley-Wilson, from the University of British Columbia in Canada, examine ICT literacies and policies in the University of British Columbia's teacher education program. The authors discuss how and what education students do with and learn about ICTs over the course of their teacher preparation program. They explore the interdependencies between new ICT standards for teachers and the politics of instrumental measures and definitions of ICT literacy and caution that conventional deficit models simplify interpretations of ICT literacy data. In the final analysis, they note that the teacher education program's ICT training for students makes only a slight difference in the students' ICT skills but reinforces instrumental literacies, including perceptions that technology is just a tool.

In Chapter Eight, Tracey Leacock from Simon Fraser University in Canada ponders the question of why so many ICT projects in schools have not lived up to their great expectations. She examines how an understanding of human decision making processes might help guide administrators and instructors in making better decisions about ICTs in the future and how improving the decision making process for technology might increase the benefits of ICT use in higher education.

In Chapter Nine, Tony Di Petta, Vera Woloshyn, and John Novak from Brock University in Canada offer an invitational education perspective on the nature of the issues and concerns associated with ICT as presented by a group of teacher-candidates preparing for their educational careers. The authors also present an invitational checklist designed to promote discussion of technology integration that both technophiles and technopragmatists alike will appreciate as a "prudent" re-mapping of the role of information and communication technology in schools. They remind us that mapping the landscape of technology is never quite the same as living the landscape experientially.

The authors of *The Emperor's New Computer* have all contributed to looking behind the curtain separating the hype from the reality of ICT use in education. Whatever the technological fashion may be from this point forward, the moral of *The Emperor's New Computer* is that educators, researchers, and everyone drawn to ICT's seductive light must pragmatically look for what lies behind the fashion and ask, "What can this technology do for teachers, learners, and education, and what will it cost?"

Tony Di Petta
Brock University
Canada

1. TEACHERS, TEACHING, SCHOOLS, AND SOCIETY

Lessons from the Philosophy of Technology

There has developed since around the end of the Second World War, a body of writing that has become known as the *Philosophy of Technology*. This writing now includes work by those who can be identified as "seminal thinkers," as well as developments of their original ideas, and fresh work and commentary on specific issues, to produce what is now a quite wide ranging body of literature. This chapter is primarily a descriptive one that summarizes the general field with an eye to its significance for teaching and teachers, highlighting some perennial issues in educational thought and practice that the literature of Philosophy of Technology invites us to revisit. We are, however, also invited to reconsider a perennial debate in education, one that originates in the dialogues between Socrates and the Sophists of Classical Greece and which can be understood in terms of many of the themes of Philosophy of Technology, and of this volume. Moreover, it suggests why that debate must be re-engaged in societies governed by advanced technology, and how the activity of teaching and the role of the teacher as a "reflective practitioner" are critical factors in that re-engagement. Thus, description provides the background for both analytic and critical dimensions of the Chapter.

THE PHILOSOPHY OF TECHNOLOGY

Stimulated by reflection on the nature and scale of the carnage of both World Wars, a number of writers provided the stimulus and some deep insights for what is now understood as a domain or field of inquiry that is Philosophy of Technology. The field is variously characterized and defined, as, indeed, is *technology* itself, and no simple definition will satisfy everyone. However, in terms of Pellegrino and Thomasma's (1981) interesting differentiation between philosophy *and*, *in*, and *of* a particular field (medicine in their case) we could say the following. Philosophy *and* technology refers to collaborative efforts by the two fields or "disciplines" to enlarge the consideration of common problems. Here, philosophical analysis of the concept of intelligent behavior might assist and be assisted by knowledge of what was actually possible in regard to making "intelligent machines." Philosophy *in* technology is the application of philosophy in its different modes (analytic, synthetic, speculative, critical) to a particular issue or problem in technology or its use. Here, ethical questions in the use of technology represent an example.

Finally, philosophy *of* technology is the critical analysis of technology as a practice or collection of practices. What will be in focus here are the theories and ideologies concerning it or expressed in the arguments for its use or non-use in particular fields, the conceptual dimensions (for example, the definition of

T. Di Petta (Ed.), The Emperor's New Computer: ICT, Teachers and Teaching, 5–16.

"technology" itself), and the philosophical basis of ethical reasoning applied to those practices. It will take the two general lines that are seen in all "philosophies of," that is, on the one hand efforts to say what technology "is" – substantively not only conceptually – and, on the other hand, what it ought to be or how it ought to be conducted, managed, or controlled. The existing literature goes to all of these different ways of engaging technology with philosophy, though Philosophy of Technology remains relatively under developed by contrast to philosophy of science, art, education, and so forth.

Three very significant thinkers who can be rightly called seminal thinkers of this field – without detracting from many other laborers in it – are Herbert Marcuse (1898-1979), Martin Heidegger (1889-1976), and Jacques Ellul (1912-1994). It is their work that early expressed different critical perspectives on the phenomenon that was life in societies governed by advanced technology. In turn, a number of thinkers developed the ideas raised in the early work through descriptive or synthetic discussion, critical reflection, and alternative analyses of their ideas; for example, Tesconi and Morris (1972), Jonas (1974), Durbin (1976), Ihde (1979), Rapp (1982), Feenberg (1991, 1995, 1999), Mitcham (1994), and Waks (1995), to mention but a few.

In the most general terms, what emerges from this writing is concern about the negative influence of technology even in the face of undoubted benefits of it. Initially, Ellul (1954/1964) and, later, also Jones (1982), were content to "awaken the sleeper," that is, to urge and assist us to look past the benefits to the wider and deeper individual and social consequences. Subsequently, a body of literature was to grow and develop to create a situation where there is a wealth of reflection available to us. It is fitting to start by briefly reviewing these seminal thinkers.

Marcuse (1941) wrote one of the earliest pieces that took a critical look at technology; his later work extended this early reflection (1955/1969; 1964/1970). Marcuse (1941) argued that new criteria of rationality and of individuality were being generated by advanced technology. In regard to the individual, the idea of a "subject of certain fundamental standards and values which no external authority was suppose to encroach on" (p. 415) was replaced by a system-defined individuality in which "distinctions in aptitude, insight and knowledge are transformed into different quanta of skill and training" which are marshalled and managed in terms of "performance" criteria (p. 417). Later, he went on to characterise a society that had neutralized conflict, a uni-dimensional society inhabited by uni-dimensional people all thinking and acting in an essentially homogeneous way, but unaware if it: "the overpowering machine of education and entertainment unites [the individual] with all others in a state of anaesthesia from which all detrimental ideas tend to be excluded" (Marcuse, 1964/1970, p. 91). Earlier, Marcuse (1955/1969) had discussed how the forces of Eros could allow a cohesive society to function. He illuminates how that *particular* society that is advanced technological society effects the "sleight of hand" whereby people throw in their lot with "the system," blindly accepting that they must do this or that in order that human civilization can continue, when in fact their required thought and behavior ensures the survival not of civilization but of that *particular form* of social arrangements that is, now, advanced technological society. This particular form of social arrangement creates "false needs" which we blindly praise it for satisfying, and for the apparent freedoms it distributes. These freedoms are, however, merely apparent. They operate under what he calls "repressive tolerance," which allows dissent only in so far as it is ineffectual and which channels real opposition into "neutralising" modes of expression.

Ellul (1954/1964), who uses the term *technique* to capture the dynamic nature of his quarry, described a shift in technology from it being a "fragmented ensemble of techniques," to a *structuring, organizing factor* in society. The collection of "ways of doing" (technical know-how, "knacks," tools) to which previous historical actors had access, becomes rather a force that orders our lives in terms of technical needs. Ellul (1977/1980) goes further and now moves to an idea of a *system*, one in which everything is in interaction and nothing untouched by technology: industry interacts with transport interacts with education interacts with telecommunications interacts with health interacts with leisure; the common denominator being advanced technology. He details a qualitative increase in the impact of technology, which is no longer something we use – voluntarily or robotically – but rather the very environment in which we live. Moreover, this system, he argues, is now *self-augmenting*, going on without decisive human intervention. Finally, Ellul (1988/1990) exposes the operation of the discourse about technology wherein contradictions are obscured and things that ought be questioned go not only unchallenged, but are also so entrenched as to be *unchallengeable*. This has echoes of Marcuse's (1964/1970) discussion of our blindness to contradictions involved in expressions like "deluxe fallout shelter" or "clean bomb." Ellul (1988/1990) adds a more core expression to the list: the notion of a "technical culture" is itself a contradiction!

Heidegger's (1977) work is particularly challenging, focusing as it does on *techne* as a way of *knowing* in the ancient Greek world, by contrast to modern understandings of technology – which term is derived from this techne – which stresses *doing* or *action*. For Heidegger, techne was practical knowledge, knowledge derived in our encounters with the world and its objects. He argues that in early Greek times the word techne was linked with the word *episteme*. These terms, with others, were terms for "knowing," in the widest sense of the word.

> They mean to be entirely at home in something, to understand and be expert in it. ... *techne* is a mode of *aletheuein* [truth]. ... Thus what is decisive in *techne* does not lie at all in making and manipulating nor in the using of means, but rather in the revealing. (Heidegger, p. 13)

Heidegger (1954/1966) also makes a distinction that is pertinent here, that between *meditative thinking* and *calculative thinking*, and he expresses concern that the latter is becoming and may become all that we know in social life governed by advanced technology. Calculative thinking is means-end thinking, and *puzzle*-solving focused on controlling nature, whereas meditative thinking is an engagement of the world in its own terms to learn from it, and to deal with real *problems*. His fear was that technology too easily "beguiled, bewitched, and dazzled" us, such that we come to

7

see calculative thinking as the only worthwhile form of thinking. Fromm's (1956/1963, p. 64) distinction between *intelligence*, with which humankind manipulates the world, and *reason*, with which humankind tries to understand the world, makes a similar point.

Modern day life, governed by advanced technology, celebrates calculative thinking and intelligence, rather than meditative thinking and reason, and it sees our attention focused on the relatively superficial in life, the mundane concerns of daily living. Thus are we caught-up in what Heidegger refers to as the "particulars" of life, and distracted from more significant issues; that is, from the "universal" questions of life and Life. These last go to the question of our *Being* (what is it to *Be)*, whereas life in advanced technological society centres on *being*. It is around the questions of Being where the real problems occur.

Beyond these seminal thinkers, in an account that argues for a *critical theory of technology*, Feenberg (1991) provides a valuable overview and identifies three theoretical perspectives on technology that nicely summarises the field as he sees it. One perspective is *instrumental theory*, which is as an optimistic account that argued the benefits of technology and its "neutrality." This is a conservative position, one that was less challenged by perceived problems and saw any problems caused by technology as solvable by yet other technologies. Further, there is an acceptance that technology will always be compliant with or obedient to broader human values. By contrast, for *substantive theory* technology was seen, in Ellul's terms, as a self-augmenting cultural force, a force in its own right not any longer in any significant way subject to human control. Finally, there is *critical theory* that critiques the impacts of advanced technology, but argues that technology can be controlled and that this can and ought be done democratically; technology is neither completely neutral nor totally autonomous. In later work Feenberg (1995, 1999) develops his ideas as to how technology, no less than other human activities like education and economic life, can be subjected to open debate and alternative ways of construal.

Two areas of discussion will suffice for our present descriptive purpose to further illustrate the nature and range of Philosophy of Technology. The first is a set of early papers asking whether there were any interesting philosophical questions in technology. The second concerns technology and religion.

Durbin (1976) and Black (1976) asked the first question, and Bunge (1976) answered in the affirmative. The definition of technology aside (not an easy question with answers ranging from matters of "tool making and use," across "the practical arts," to a social-structuring dynamic, to a self-augmenting system with little decisive human intervention) the three writers provide an early discussion of the legitimacy of a field now called Philosophy of Technology. One issue in contention is the question of whether there are different philosophical questions raised by technology, or whether old questions take on a new urgency. For example, the question of whether it is ever right to kill a person may be no different than when asked by the Classical Greeks, but it may have different significance at a time when it is possible to kill millions at a time. The discussion engaged by these three writers went to such things as the relationship between technology and science in a world dominated by technology (is technology "applied science," or is science now at the service of technology?); the epistemological status of technological knowledge (the type of truth claims made in science and in technology; whether technological knowledge is "knowledge" in an epistemological sense); and the ontological status of technological artefacts (does something I make and use have something of me in it?).

The second area of discussion that is illustrative of the breadth of the domain under attention here is religion. Initial interest within Christianity was in the impact of technology on the quality of Christian life where Christians were advised to be watchful and alert. Beyond that, there was a focus on values that for the Christian did not change, and the view that a crisis occurs because "too much confidence is placed in the automatic nature of purely technical solutions, while fundamental human values are forgotten" (Gremillion, 1976, p. 601). That said, however, a provocative early discussion centred on Christianity's role in the environmental crisis was White's (1967) challenge. This was that the environmental crisis was in a major way the responsibility of western Christianity and its construal of the creation story in the Bible. Thus Genesis was taken as sanctioning *domination* of nature (Genesis 1: 26/28) rather than the mere *stewardship* of nature (Genesis: 2:15). Further, reference to non-mainstream Christianity is equally interesting; technology was a key issue in the differentiation of particular groups from the mainstream, and from each other. Thus, the Amish reject technology, the Hutterites use it "with care," while the Mennonites use it "at will."

Non-Christian positions cannot be ignored and a few can be mentioned, albeit superficially. Judaism has rules about activities that may be performed on the Sabbath, including working and writing, such that technological activity on the Sabbath can be a problem. The rules going to food preparation under modern conditions of food technology and food production have also posed problems. Islam preserved Greek learning through the Dark Ages and led the world in technology until the 1500s, the Koran encouraging inquiry and learning, but science and technology are always to be evaluated in terms of how they contribute to or detract from social harmony and the quality of social life. There is a particular problem with "technology transfer" in that the acceptance of knowledge may encourage also an acceptance of other social or cultural ideas and practices. The oldest religion, Hinduism, has an interesting perspective on genetic engineering because of the belief in Karma which would signal caution in too much technological interference in correcting congenital problems. Finally, Buddhism would be expected to be critical of the waste of time in trivial pursuits, and the distractions of our minds from reflection and meditation.

Doctrinal religion aside, it is possible to argue that the "religious attitude" offers an antidote to a "technological consciousness." These two concepts may raise problems, but what is in mind is this. A religious attitude (Dewey, 1934) is concerned with *ideals*; when people live in accordance with ideals they are expressing "the religious." Thus, the "religious outlook" might serve to question technology, and offer an "antidote," even if doctrinal positions do not.

Finally, it is useful to note that the concerns raised by these earlier thinkers continue to attract attention in present times across similar fields, though with different emphases. For example, Hertz (2002) discusses how "silent conversion" of the whole world to a "global business civilization," made possible through advanced technology, corrupts the idea and the workings of democracy. Saul (2001) argues a need to rebalance, to find an equilibrium among common, shared qualities of human beings, our shared humanity. Thus might those qualities which do generate acquisitiveness and control of nature, and encourage diviseness, be kept in check by those that emphasize equally as much such qualities as common sense, ethics, intuition, and reason, which encourage cohesion. Such a balance would allow us to look forward with hope rather than despair and Saul (2005) is more optimistic for a resurgence of our humanity. This last work argues how "globalization" contains the seeds of its own destruction, and the idea that human beings are simply and easily "malleable" that is taken for granted in advanced technological society, may be a significantly wrong assumption. Thus, too, the impacts of advanced technology on culture and values continue to attract discussion. Contemporary sociologists are urged to "know technology" so as to better "know ourselves" (Matthewman, 2007), and Foucault's "technology of the body" continues to be a focus of interest in discussion of such things as eating disorders, plastic surgery, and body sculpting (West-Newman, 2007). Further, Shilling and Mellor (2007) have extended this focus and discuss "body pedagogics" as the means by which a culture transmits its "corporeal techniques, skills, dispositions and beliefs, the experiences typically associated with acquiring these attributes, and the actual *embodied changes* resulting from this process" (p. 533). Shilling and Mellor consider, too, the place of two religious traditions (Taosim and fundamentalist Christianity) in providing something of a resistance to or rethinking of these imperatives. Thus are the themes raised by earlier thinkers still "alive and well."

TECHNOLOGY, TEACHING, AND EDUCATING

Educational thinkers in the 1960s picked-up a mood that expressed an unease with the increasing dominance of teaching, schooling, and education, by technology, sometimes aided and abetted – if not orchestrated – by the demands of "business;" this unease appears no less strong at the present time. To take the last point first, that is, the issue of business, John Dewey (1929/1962) had earlier expressed significant reservations about too keen an interest in education by business interests. His concern was to arrest the destructive impact of money and a "business ideology" on a sense of social cohesion and shared purpose, and his role in Progressive Education was significantly motivated by this loss of "community" he saw at that time. Related, was Callahan's (1962) discussion of the "concept of efficiency," which reveals the extent to which educational administrators in the early 1900s privileged ideas about how best to manage, schools – the "how" of it all – over the broader educational aims of schooling, the "why" of it all.

However, Tesconi and Morris perhaps best captured in summary form the critical writing on technology and its link to education, drawing on the earlier thinkers whose ideas were sketched above. Their title is instructive for the intensity of the negative appraisal they discuss; that is, *The Anti-man Culture* (1972). They coin the term *bureautechnocracy* to describe the new social culture in which "a pyramidal hierarchy of operational control [bureaucracy] is linked with rationalized and standardized means for reaching predetermined ends [technology], with the overall aim of achieving systematisation, efficiency, and economy" (p. 161), and go on to summarize the outcomes. Their summary highlights a range of individual and social consequences drawn from the writing with which we began, and other analyses. For example, (a) the shift to "mass society" in which an idea of "community" (shared purpose, cohesive, qualitative grouping) is lost in that of "society" (instrumental purposes, conflict, quantitative grouping); (b) a general homogenisation which values sameness and conformity; (c) the thwarting of social change; (d) alienation and the growth of a class of "experts;" (e) the individual's a loss of self-esteem; (f) a "re-ordering of the superego;" (g) a celebration of "freedom from" which distracts from the lack of "freedom to;" and (h) a society of surveillance.

Some of these last points require clarification, in particular the third, sixth, and last. The notion that there is no social change appears silly until Marcuse's argument is recalled. That is, that there is merely quantitative change, not qualitative change in that the structure of production and distribution has not changed since the Industrial Revolution! Again, this follows Marcuse, who works with the Freudian structure of personality and the concept of the *superego* as imposing the demands of civilized life. Thus, freedom from restraint as a feature of modern life – the restraints of toil, of dogma, of arbitrary treatment by the State – has little meaning if people do not know what to do with their newfound "freedom from;" that is, do not have "freedom to." Moreover, such previous social demands (superego) as "save now and have it later," change to "have it now and pay later." Finally, a society of surveillance sees unprecedented means of watching and gathering information on the citizenry, but, more importantly, a sense of each of us continuously "having to give an account" of ourselves, a conscious and unconscious sense of needing to "measure up" and "keep up."

Later writers turned more specific attention the matter of technology, work, and education and their ideas will emerge throughout this volume. In passing, though, it is worth noting Feinberg and Rosemont's (1975) collection. They gathered ideas from significant educational thinkers addressing a range of matters including authority in education (whether based in technology or in community; Kenneth Benne), the submergence of individual interests in the social (Joel Spring), art and technology as alternate models of education (Mark Wartofsky), a phenomenology of man-machine relations (Don Ihde), and the need to recapture a humanistic conception of education (Naom Chomsky). Waks's (1995) reflections, two decades later, pursue similar themes, though more comprehensively in regard to education "writ large."

These observations made, it is finally of value to change direction and note that the relationship between teaching and technology goes back in the history of education a very long way, not superficially but more fundamentally. That is, the relationship is not only about what tools were used to assist an activity of teaching or educating, but can be considered in terms of how teaching and education were construed in their "essence." This is captured over a quarter of a century ago in Brumbaugh's (1973) discussion where he makes a number of highly pertinent observations, including the identification of a way of construing education itself as a "simple technology." It is most instructive here to review his discussion.

Brumbaugh (1973) distinguishes three conceptions of what education is all about, one of these now considerably rare, though not completely absent in our world. The rare one he calls "education as fantasy", the more familiar ones, "education as understanding," and "education as simple technology." Education as fantasy is characterized by the idea of providing young people – any people – with a story in song or epic poem or a book. Then, we have them immerse themselves uncritically in that story which has in it all of the elements they need to know for community life, the rituals and the "truths" of social living. Then, further, we expose them to examples of those who have lived the story; thus, through emulation, they will grow and develop in terms of the story. His example is ancient Greece where the "book" was Homer and the exemplars were the heroes of a noble warrior culture. This perspective on education would be difficult to locate today, except in some fundamentalist religious communities.

The second notion of education, more relevant here, is education as simple technology. The activity of education and the practice of teaching were understood as a process in which something was "done to" a student, particular information "transmitted." It was the Sophists of classical Greece who first epitomized this outlook and this practice. Education was the learning of material and techniques for "getting on" in life. At that time such subjects included rhetoric, for a social context in which one represented oneself in public life and in legal disputes, as well as social etiquette, and "skills and bits of cultural information." Brumbaugh suggest that the Sophists were not overly curious about the nature of the *self*, and their learning theory was based on the model of a machine that stored information for retrieval. Retrieval was facilitated using techniques that they invented and taught, such as mnemonics, and practices such as quiz programs and the use of reference books. This was "an approach that emphasized skill, information, conditioned conformity … [and] a total inability to grasp inductive generalization" (1973, p. 10). Doniela (1972) in his discussion specifically of the nature of the University, draws a similar distinction as does Brumbaugh, but notes the two-sidedness of the instrumental view epitomized by the Sophists. This is that there can be now seen a conservative and a radical arm of such a view. The one, the conservative, sees the function of education as conserving tradition and passing on traditional knowledge and skill. The second, however, sees the function of education as creating those informed and clearer sighted cadres that will change the existing system. For Doniela, whether seeking to "pass on" accepted and acceptable knowledge, or preparing young people to change things in a particular direction, or, perhaps develop good interpersonal relationship skills, both the conservative and the radical-progressive are equally opposed to the next outlook.

Finally, the third conception, education as understanding, is arguably very important for contemporary education, teaching, and learning. This view of education sees it as an activity aimed at understanding not techniques and tricks of argument, or having an encyclopedic store of information at one's mental fingertips, but understanding general principles. Thus, "from Socrates through Plato and Aristotle, the conviction was shared that the aim of education is the kind of 'freedom' that comes from understanding general principles, causes, and sequences" (Brumbaugh, 1973, p. 11).

Brumbaugh (1973) aligns each of these last two conceptions of education with a metaphysical principle, which he argues underpins it. Underpinning education as simple technology is a "metaphysic of limitation," and for education as understanding a "metaphysic of plenitude." A metaphysic of limitation stresses an underlying reality in which individual things conform to types, and commonality and form are what are of interest. By contrast, a metaphysic of limitation focuses the fact that any individual thing will always vary from its strict typology, that "concrete individuals are more than mere type-outlines in space and time, infinitely more, and that this greater complexity gives them an added dimension of aesthetic interest" (p. 8).

Brumbaugh (1973) argued that a revolution in education required a change in the underlying view of reality, the underlying metaphysic. He argued that a systematic change was needed and that this needed to be done systematically, which, in turn, meant that it had to be planned philosophically; only through philosophy can we get to "the higher levels of generality of the system, and judge their adequacy by the degree to which they are realistic." This judgment needed both "philosophical analysis and metaphysical speculation, since to determine what is or is not realistic requires a prior knowledge of what is real" (p. 7).

This discussion of education as simple technology is interesting for a view put over a quarter of a century ago at a conference in Scotland on technology and education. Hubbard (1983) observed that the early days of an economic and social revolution were in evidence and that one thing that this meant was "an end to any view which separated education and training" (p. 9). The argument offered for such view was in terms of the needs of society having to be balanced with the needs of the individual and we were reminded that "we have a universal public system of education largely because of a need for a minimum standard of education in the industrial workforce" (p. 9). The present discussion would not support education as totally devoid of practical considerations or overly focused on philosophy. It would stress that *vocational education* ought not become the vocationalisation of education, and that *some* rather than *no* orientation of neophyte teachers to the philosophy, no less than the history, of education is vital.

From the brief overview of the nature and range of Philosophy of Technology provided here, this domain would appear to be a fruitful one for *all* those involved in the educational enterprise if they share the view that advanced technology has and is impacting educational thought and teaching practice in not always constructive ways. It would seem to be significant for students and for teachers to maintain a critical-skeptical outlook in the face of relentless pressures to have the system function merely to serve the interests of advanced technology. In this outlook the insights of the science, technology, and society studies field will be invaluable, provided, as Waks (1995) argues, the different "subcultures" of this field can be integrated. But it may need more than this.

CONCLUSION

If teachers, at the grassroots of the activity of education, are to move past that "sleep" that the early writers were trying to awaken us from, then two recommendations can be offered here. First, engage the literature comprising philosophy of technology. Second, re-engage the debate about the fundamental purposes of education.

The first is superficially easy and involves reflection of the type the present volume encourages. The second ought be a core aspect of teacher education guided by one of the key principles of Progressivism. That is, that education could be democratized without being vulgarized (Cremin, 1961), that the fruits of a humanistic culture could be shared by all and need not, and should not, be submerged in, or degraded by, a so called "technical culture."

We can capture what should be our concerns as teachers and educators with reference to a story from the Taoist tradition and told in Legge (1891/1962) as follows. A monk observed a man working in a garden, conveying water by means of carrying it in a jar to irrigation channels, using much energy for little result. The monk described to him a piece of simple yet ingenious technology that would make the task easier and more efficient, and could extend the amount of land that could be used. The gardener listened and then replied:

> ... where there are ingenious contrivances, there are sure to be subtle doings; and ... where there are subtle doings, there is sure to be a scheming mind. But where there is a scheming mind in the breast, its pure simplicity is impaired. When this pure simplicity is impaired, the spirit becomes unsettled, and the unsettled spirit is not the proper residence of the Tao. It is not that I do not know (the contrivance which you mention), but that I should be ashamed to use it. (pp. 319–320)

Nothing more needs to be said than this to drive home the fundamental nature of what should be our concerns.

REFERENCES

Black, M. (1976). Are there any philosophically interesting questions in technology? *Proceedings of the Philosophy of Science Association, 2*, 185–193.

Brumbaugh, R. S. (1973). Education and reality: Two revolutions. *Thought, 48*, 5–18.

Bunge, M. (1976). The philosophical richness of technology. *Proceedings of the Philosophy of Science Association, 2*, 153–172.

Callahan, R. E. (1962). *Education and the cult of efficiency*. Chicago: University of Chicago Press.

Cremin, L. A. (1961). *The transformation of the school: Progressivism in American education 1876–1957*. New York: Random House.

Dewey, J. (1934). *A common faith*. New Haven, CT: Yale University Press.

Dewey, J. (1962). *Individualism old and new*. New York: Capricorn Books. (Original work published 1929)

Doniela, B. (1972). The university: Socratic and sophistic. *Dialectic*. Australia: University of Newcastle, 7, 34–45.

Durbin, P. T. (1976). Are there interesting philosophical issues in technology as distinct from science? An overview of philosophy of technology. *Proceedings of the Philosophy of Science Association, 2*, 139–152.

Ellul, J. (1964). *The technological society* (J. Wilkinson, Trans.). London: Jonathon Cape. (Original work published 1954)

Ellul, J. (1980). *The technological system* (J. Neugroschel, Trans.). New York: Continuum. (Original work published 1977)

Ellul, J. (1990). *The technological bluff*. Grand Rapids, MI: W. B. Eerdmans. (Original work published 1988)

Feenberg, A. (1991). *Critical theory of technology*. New York: Oxford University Press.

Feenberg, A. (1995). *Alternative modernity*. Berkeley, CA: University of California Press.

Feenberg, A. (1999). *Questioning technology*. London: Routledge.

Feinberg, W., & Rosemont, H., Jr. (1975). *Work, technology and education*. Chicago: University of Chicago Press.

Fromm, E. (1963*). The sane society*. London: Routledge. (Original work published 1956)

Gremillion, J. (Ed.). (1976). *The gospel of peace and justice: Catholic social teaching since Pope John*. Maryknoll, NY: Orbit Books.

Heidegger, M. (1966). *What is called thinking?* (F. D. Wieck & J. G. Gray, Trans.). New York: Harper and Row. (Original work published 1954)

Heidegger, M. (1977). *The question concerning technology* (with an introduction by W. Lovitt, Trans.). New York: Harper and Row.

Hertz, N. (2002). *The silent takeover: Global capitalism and the death of democracy*. London: Random House.

Hubbard, G. (1983, March). Introduction: Education, training and the new technologies. In J. Tucker (Ed.), *A report of the Scottish council for educational technology conference: "Look out for learners"* (pp. 16–17). London: Kogan Page.

Ihde, D. (1979). *Technics and praxis*. Boston: D. Reidel.

Jonas, H. (Ed.). (1974). Technology and responsibility: Reflections on the new tasks of ethics. In *Philosophical essay: From ancient creed to technological mans* (pp. 115–126). New York: Prentice Hall.

Jones, B. (1982). *Sleepers wake! Technology and the future of work*. Melbourne, Australia: Oxford University Press.

Legge, J. (1962). The texts of Taoism. In F. M. Muller (Ed.), *The sacred books of the east* (Vol. 39, pp. 47–123). New York: Dover. (Original work published 1891)

Marcuse, H. (1941). Some implications of modern technology. *Philosophy of Science*, 414–439.

Marcuse, H. (1969). *Eros and civilization*. London: Sphere Books. (Original work published 1955)

Marcuse, H. (1970). *One-dimensional man*. London: Sphere Books. (Original work published 1964)

Matthewman, S. (2007). Mediating: Technology. In S. Matthewman, C. L. West-Newman, & B. Curtis (Eds.), *Being sociological* (pp. 335–353). Basingstoke, Great Britain: Palgrave Macmillan.

Mitcham, C. (1994). *Thinking through technology*. Chicago: University of Chicago Press.

Pellegrino, E. D., & Thomasma, D. C. (1981). *A philosophical basis of medical practice*. Oxford: Oxford University Press.

Rapp, F. (1982). Philosophy of technology. In G. Floistad (Ed.), *Contemporary philosophy: A new survey* (Vol. 3, pp. 361–412). The Hague, The Netherlands: Martinus Nijhoff.

Saul, J. R. (2001). *On equilibrium*. New York: Penguin.

Saul, J. R. (2005). *The collapse of globalism and the reinvention of the world*. Toronto, ON: Viking Press.

Shilling, C., & Mellor, P. A. (2007). Cultures of embodied experience: Technology, religion and body pedagogics. *The Sociological Review, 55*(3), 531–549.

Tesconi, C. Jr., & Morris, V. C. (1972). *The anti-man culture: Bureautechnocracy and the schools*. Urbana, IL: University of Illinois Press.

Waks, L. J. (1995). Technology's school: The challenge to philosophy. *Research in philosophy and technology*, Suppl. 3. Greenwich, CT: JAI Press.

West-Newman, C. L. (2007). Governing: Power. In S. Matthewman, C. L. West-Newman, & B. Curtis (Eds.), *Being sociological* (pp. 149–170). Basingstoke, Great Britain: Palgrave Macmillan.

White, L., Jr. (1967). The historical roots of our ecological crisis. *Science, 55*(3767), 1203–1207.

William Warren
University of Newcastle
Australia

2. THE IMPACT OF DIGITAL TECHNOLOGIES AND THE NEED FOR TECHNOLOGICAL PEDAGOGICAL CONTENT KNOWLEDGE

Lessons from the Virtual Historian

INTRODUCTION

"Technology," as an issue of *Education Canada* (2001) – the Canadian Education Association's leading magazine – states, "has become an accepted fact of life and education." "Serious discussion of the changes that technology is making to teaching and learning," the editor goes on, "forces us to revisit some fundamental questions about the goals of schooling and the foundations of learning" (Dunning, p. 1). Indeed, computational technologies have radically altered people's working and living practices – from video-conferencing to computer gaming to online shopping. As might be expected, technological aficionados foresee similar drastic changes in educational policies, curricula, and practices – and for sound reasons. For example, the Programme for International Student Assessment (PISA) results of 2000 reveal the significant role and impact of computational technology on students' learning, particularly for western countries such as Canada. Not only is the home penetration rate of such technology for high school students extremely high (88% as of 2000), but statistics indicate a positive correlation between computer and internet access and students' literacy practices. "PISA results," Bussières and Gluszynski (2002) note in their Canadian evaluation of the study, "showed that there was a positive association between reading scores and home computer access, and this association increased with the number of computers present" (p. 17).

Yet beyond this excitement for technology in education, it is increasingly apparent in school circles that Information and Communications Technology (ICT) in its current form cannot be integrated directly into classrooms without educational transformation. Features of computer hardware and software, as well as digital technologies available to users, rarely match pedagogical demands of students and teachers. Whether it is an online program, a virtual simulation, or an interactive presentation, users must perform multiple, and often complex, adjustments to fit local curriculum requirements. For Bill Tally (2007), senior researcher at the Center for Children and Technology in New York, teachers correctly judge computers "to be too finicky and troublesome to fit in well with the demands of the school workday – in short, not worth the trouble" (p. 310).

Under the circumstances, what are the impacts of ICT on classroom teaching and students' learning? What educational technology or digital applications can improve

T. Di Petta, (Ed.), The Emperor's New Computer: ICT, Teachers and Teaching, 17–28.

learner-centred practices and disciplinary expertise? What evidence do we have that such technologies have a positive effect on schooling?

This chapter addresses some of these fundamental questions from a disciplinary perspective. Using history as a domain of knowledge, it first reviews the research base related to inquiry learning and digital technology in history education. For the purpose of this chapter, "digital technology" refers to computer or network-based applications and resources, including online learning programs, supporting teaching and learning of subject matter. Then, the chapter explores the implications of using technology in the classroom, focusing on the findings from our studies with the Virtual Historian. It then argues for the development of technological pedagogical content knowledge as an additional knowledge base for successful integration of technology in education.

DOING HISTORY...WITH TECHNOLOGY

History educators have long argued for more authentic forms of history teaching and learning. From the 19th century inquiry ideas of Leopold von Ranke through to Fred Morrow Fling's "source methods," progressive historians have believed in a theory of school history anchored in teaching the discipline with inquiry. Meaningful and enduring understanding, from this perspective, is an active and continuous process of knowledge acquisition and (re)construction in light of students' prior knowledge, understanding, and engagement. In history education, several studies (Seixas, 2002; Shemilt, 1987; Wineburg, 2001) have documented the futility of teaching historical knowledge with traditional stories about the past. Instead, they have pointed to the necessity of engaging students actively in the heuristics of reading, sourcing, researching, and doing historical investigations.

Yet, as Wineburg (2001) puts it so eloquently, historical thinking is not a "natural" act (p. 7). It is a sophisticated form of knowledge. Novices intuitively view history as a story of the past whereas historians develop expertise in thinking critically about the past. For the former, learning history is equated to "getting the story right," usually in the form of a simplified narrative as found in textbooks. For the latter, however, knowing history implies a complex – and always tentative – dialogue with the past using available evidence and tools of the discipline.

Faced with this situation, Wineburg (2001) believes that teachers must engage students in sophisticated thinking. To do so, teachers need (a) deep understanding of their discipline, and (b) successful instructional strategies and pertinent pedagogies that support active learning and thinking in the classroom. Growing evidence suggests that development of a community of inquiry can help develop expertise among novices (Bain, 2006; Friedman, 2006; Levstik & Barton, 2001; VanSledright, 2002). Levstik and Barton indicate that the history process of asking meaningful questions, finding evidence, and drawing conclusions is known as inquiry. Teachers, they argue, "can capitalize on children's natural enthusiasm for learning by making their classrooms places where students explore important and meaningful questions" (p. 13).

Such inquiry learning strategies in the domain, however, pose significant challenges to educators. For Seixas (1993), the community of inquiry in the classroom does not – and cannot – replicate that of the historian's. Given age fundamental differences, experience and relation to knowledge and authorities, the classroom community of inquiry is rather a place where "history teachers occupy a key position between two communities organised around history knowledge and learning" (p. 319). Students only form a community of inquiry if they are introduced to inquiries "under the skillful direction of a teacher" (p. 320). Indeed, as studies reveal, the development of expertise in history must be based on sound pedagogy that "value[s] inquiry deeply to undertake the challenges of such demanding practice" (Saye & Brush, 2006a, p. 184).

Potential benefits of building a community of inquiry in the history classroom are many. It provides teachers with experience and understanding of what it means to do history and how students can progress toward more sophisticated thinking. From this perspective, as VanSledright (2004) contends, historians can serve as a "benchmark in relationship to which we can understand what the less sophisticated historical thinkers do" (p. 230). Second, a community of inquiry creates a learning environment more conducive to students' discovery – a key aspect of constructivist learning. The community of inquiry puts students in charge of their own learning and engages them in authentic performances. Finally, building a community of inquiry necessitates a different learning interaction with the subject-matter. Because students do not intuitively know how to think critically, they must count on the support of teachers. Teachers must model best practices by demonstrating what it is like to inquire, that is, to investigate the past using essential questions, to collect and analyze evidence, and to draw conclusions and make judgements. On the other hand, coaching students implies another key element of inquiry-based learning: scaffolding. Because students need support to progress in the discipline, teachers must provide the necessary learning structure. By breaking down investigative activity into smaller, more manageable components and by offering scaffolds, it becomes possible for students to engage progressively in meaningful inquires.

Equally challenging is the use of educational technologies. I have argued elsewhere that rich technological open learning environments, such as digital history programs, can support inquiry-based learning because of the types of materials and opportunities they offer to users (Lévesque, 2006). With development of the internet and related applications, there has been a push in the last decade to infuse digital technology into the curriculum (Swan & Hofer, 2008). As Saye and Brush (2006a) argue, digital open learning environments (a) create more realistic, vivid engagement with history (life-like inquiries) than what is currently available, and (b) draw on and stimulate student development of expertise in history and new technologies.

While school subjects such as science, language arts, and geography directly benefit from the affordances of instructional technologies, history lags behind (see Cohen & Rosenzweig, 2005; Saye & Brush, 2007). Particularly in Canadian education, few digital programs are geared toward history education beyond archival websites, virtual tours and online texts. The recent development of *Great Unsolved*

Mysteries in Canadian History (http://www.canadianmysteries.ca) and the *Cyberterrorism Crisis Web Site* (see Chapter 3 in this book) present refreshing initiatives to Canadian educators (see Sandwell, 2005). In their own unique way, these programs put users in the virtual shoes of detectives engaged in investigating past and contemporary issues of significance.

STUDENTS' LEARNING AND THE VIRTUAL HISTORIAN

Instructional experience and effectiveness of digital technology directly affect student learning. Studies have revealed the limited pedagogical impact of story-telling on students' historical development and reasoning (Voss & Wiley, 2000; Yeager & Doppen, 2001). As they are not exposed to what it means to do history, students typically see themselves as passive receivers whose role is to "get the story right." There is thus a need for a shift in students' existing habits of classroom work. The integration of technology in the history classroom can provide a catalyst for such a change (Ashburn, Baildon, Damico, & McNair, 2006).

Yet, educators must not hold unrealistic expectations. Recent findings in education suggest that technology alone is no panacea (DeWitt, 2007; Friedman, 2006; Tally, 2007). Friedman argues in his study of high school history teachers and technology that the use of online sources "depended to a greater extent on their access to computer projectors and school computing facilities..." (p. 139). In the same way, the experimental studies of Saye and Brush (2004, 2006a, 2006b, 2007) and Britt, Perfetti, Van Dyke, and Gabrys (2000), the qualitative works of Lee and Calandra (2004) and Milson (2002) on WebQuest, and finally the Google study of Pan et al. (2007) offer important recommendations to consider. Affordable access to online resources, such as primary source documents and artefacts, provide users with a rich base of historical information rarely available in textbooks and learning guides. From such sources, students can be exposed to a greater variety of source types (print, audio, video, and artifactual) and perspectives on a given subject, widening their horizons and increasing their understanding of history. Yet, many students in these studies have expressed concerns with regard to the nature of the sources and the amount of sources available. Online texts – digitized historical ones in particular – are rarely produced in a language and genre familiar to students in their textbooks. In the same way, the large amount of information available at the click of the mouse seems to overwhelm students who lack searching and skimming skills necessary to navigate multiple, and often contradictory, texts. The end result, as Milson (2002) observes, is that many students typically adopt a "path-of-least-resistance," scanning the material for quick and easy cut-and-paste factual answers (p. 344).

Finally, learning scaffolds provided to students offer interactive cognitive tools meant to support learners as they engage in doing history. These learning supports (e.g., worksheets, heuristic questions, writing templates, definitions, and answers) facilitate inquiry skills, literacy, and historical reasoning. But results suggest that scaffolds are not necessarily used by students who rely on their intuitive thinking, which leads them to briefly search texts for the "right story," and not engage in the analytic process of reading historical sources.

Available to users in both French and English, the Virtual Historian (VH) (www.virtualhistorian.ca) is an educational technology developed to meet some of the challenges of digital history learning (see Figure 1). Unlike texts, learning guides and WebQuests, the VH provides users with non-linear, authentic, and realistic inquiries ("missions") about key issues in Canadian history. Web-based inquiries are framed around "topical questions," which call for critical analysis, dialectical reasoning, and sophisticated understanding of central phenomena in the history curriculum (Wiggins & McTighe, 2005, p. 113). To complete the inquiries, students are provided with an online tutorial, a brief synopsis of the "mission" with a topical question to answer, curriculum rubrics presenting all learning objectives addressed in the mission, some conflicting primary and secondary sources on the issue (including high resolution digitized copies of originals that can be manipulated online), embedded reading, sourcing, and writing scaffolds to support thinking and active learning, and a web-based notepad to record and write answers. Students have access to an online glossary, additional web resources (e.g., national archives, museums, and newspapers) as well as to an integrated email program to communicate with the teacher or program administrator.

Figure 1. The Virtual Historian library (October Crisis, 1970)

Even though the VH was designed to promote inquiry learning, does it really work? Does it have a positive impact on students' sophisticated understanding? To answer these questions, two experimental studies were conducted with Ontario high school students in 2006 and 2007. Following the Canadian history curriculum for Grade 10 (Ontario Ministry of Education, 2005), two missions (cases) were developed in the VH program: one history case on the "FLQ and the October Crisis of 1970" with two Grade 10 history classes (one instructional and one VH), and one case on "World War II and the Dieppe Raid, 1942" with four Grade 10 history classes (two instructional and two VH) from two different school boards. By using the VH in Canadian classrooms, studies aimed to uncover the still unclear role and influence of such educational technology on students' historical thinking and literacy – in terms of knowledge acquisition, procedural understanding (e.g., use of evidence, perspective, moral judgement), and epistemological knowledge understanding (how historical knowledge is constructed). Because of its potential, the assumption was that digital history, as built in the VH program, can "*mediate* and *support* students' historical thinking" (Bain, 2006, p. 109).

Table 1. Mean scores and standard deviations for each variable by group

Variables	Instructional Groups			Virtual Historian Groups		
	Pre-test mean (SD)	Post-test mean (SD)	Essay mean (SD)	Pre-test mean (SD)	Post-test mean (SD)	Essay mean (SD)
Tests and essay (October Crisis)	2.17 (1.20)	9.81 (2.41)	8.64 (4.43)	4.12 (2.47)	12.45 (1.32)	14.80 (2.52)
Meta-cognition (October Crisis)		2.30 (0.88)			2.86 (0.88)	
Tests and essay School board #1 (WWII – Dieppe)	3.51 (1.17)	10.29 (2.65)	12.26 (3.69)	3.94 (1.78)	11.51 (2.60)	15.93 (2.89)
Meta-cognition School board #1 (WWII – Dieppe)		3.53 (1.38)			4.23 (1.59)	
Tests and essay School board #2 (WWII – Dieppe)	4.11 (2.67)	9.08 (2.60)	12.55 (2.58)	3.72 (2.76)	10.57 (2.45)	12.73 (4.03)
Meta-cognition School board #2 (WWII – Dieppe)		2.99 (1.71)			4.38 (1.58)	

Table 1 presents data on the VH and comparison groups concerning their understanding of subject matter, discipline, and metacognition for each history case (October Crisis; World War II and the Dieppe Raid). For both groups, students increased their comprehension of the subject-matter, understanding of history, and literacy skills (ability to write an argumentative essay). However, using the VH led to the organization and writing of more sophisticated essays in both history cases. Students in the VH groups were able to construct more structured and coherent arguments than their counterparts. Their knowledge of the subject (e.g., series of events, actors, facts) was greater and their ability to think historically (present clear arguments supported by appropriate evidence, consider historical significance, and make judgement on the issue) was significantly more sophisticated than those in the instructional groups. Students in the VH group also developed more advanced meta-conceptual awareness of self-learning and achievement. An examination of standard deviations of post-test scores between the VH groups and the comparison groups also suggests more constant results among students in the VH groups. The standard deviations of the essay scores show the same pattern, except for school board no. 2. These results indicate that responses from students in the former groups were not as widely dispersed as in the comparison groups, and were thus closer to the mean score, indicating that the digital program helped produce more consistently positive outcomes among students of the VH groups.

DISCUSSION: THE NEED FOR TECHNOLOGICAL PEDAGOGICAL CONTENT KNOWLEDGE (TPCK)

There has been a tendency in computational technology literature to blend critical research with self-advocacy. Supporters of new technologies in education tend to see the positive impact in the market place as an indicator of their uncontested potential for classroom improvement. These people, as Swan and Hofer (2008) argue, "appear to assume that technology is preferable to traditional modes of instruction, that it can make a good teacher better, and that it leads to more student-centered (and therefore preferable) instruction" (p. 321). Findings from the VH studies suggest a positive impact of the program on student achievement. As one experimental group student puts it, "It's way better than reading from a textbook or other websites you can't be sure of." Another student goes further by arguing that "instead of being taught the topic, we learned it without [teacher] support, which I think helped me more in overall knowledge."

In light of students' appreciation and performance, one could advocate for a greater place for such digital technology in the classroom. Yet, the educational community will be better served in the end if researchers look at how specific educational technologies affect students and how digital programs such as the VH support or detract from particular kinds of learning and achievement. Instead of presenting narrowly defined case studies of best practices or new technology implementation, it may be worth analyzing both the potentials and challenges of integrating educational technology in history education. As a matter of fact, the studies with the VH – as well as other digital programs – present challenges that are critical for further use in the classroom.

Indeed, while most students who exclusively used the VH program increased their overall understanding of history significantly, the great majority continued to look at historical sources from a "readerly" perspective (Wineburg, 2001, p. 69). Texts – whether they are print, visual, audiovisual, or artifactual – are examined exclusively for their conventional, straightforward messages, not for the subtexts and contextualized meaning they convey. Primary sources are comparable to textbooks in that they contain answers ("facts") that must be discovered. They fail to understand the constructed nature of texts and the purpose and perspective of the authors. More problematic, they attribute greater importance and reliability to simplified secondary sources, such as textbooks, because they convey intelligible conventional truths. As one student confesses, "in class reading a textbook is better because its very hard to find accurate info on the computer."

Similarly, over 60 percent of students in our studies reported in the post-test preferring either classroom teaching or a combination of teacher-computer to the VH program alone. Reasons given range from the familiarity with the teacher's style, the unchallenging nature of classroom lectures, the difficulty to navigate and analyze multiple texts (even with scaffolds), deep confidence in simplified textbook stories, and finally classroom interactions with the teacher, students, and learning objects. For this student, "I personally prefer learning Canadian history in class because we go through it and you don't need to look for your own information." For another student, "its better in the lab, because it's more fun; however, it is distracting."

The experimental studies with the VH were designed to assess the value of a digital history program on students' performance. The role of the teacher was therefore restricted significantly in the computer lab so as to limit – and ultimately control – this variable. In reality, however, classroom teachers have a greater role to play in the design, implementation, and delivery of lessons – whether they rely on educational technology or not. "It is important to remember," Bain (2006) cautiously observes, "that computer scaffolding does not substitute for instruction, but rather supports students in developing disciplinary habits after they have had at least initial instruction in each procedure" (p. 113).

To be sure, expertise in teaching a discipline, whether history or science, depends on access to and use of complex systems of knowledge. Shulman (1986) established that disciplinary knowledge and pedagogy were necessary but not sufficient conditions to render a subject intelligible to students. Pedagogical content knowledge, he argued, is of special interest to teachers because "it represents the blending of content and pedagogy into an understanding of how particular topics, problems, or issues are organized, represented, and adapted to the diverse interests and abilities of learners, and presented for instruction" (Shulman, p. 8). While Shulman's pedagogical ideas still hold true today, the rapid development and application of educational technologies in the classroom necessitates a review of his teaching model.

Indeed, not all teachers embrace technology – for a variety of personal and professional reasons – but the growing presence of technology in education is uncontested. As such, it becomes imperative to revisit the relation between content, pedagogy, and technology. Too often, knowledge of technology in education is considered in a vacuum, disconnected from disciplinary knowledge and pedagogy, as if an understanding of how technological affordances work translates into sound practice. Students' and teachers' familiarity with technology does not automatically turn them into disciplinary experts. For Mishra and Koehler (2006), there is thus a need to develop "technological pedagogical content knowledge" (TPCK) as a basis for teaching with all three forms of knowledge (see Figure 2). This kind of knowledge, they argue:

> is the basis of good teaching with technology and requires an understanding of the representation of concepts using technologies; pedagogical techniques that use technologies in constructive ways to teach content; knowledge of what makes concepts difficult or easy to learn and how technology can help redress some of the problems that students face; knowledge of students' prior knowledge and theories of epistemology; and knowledge of how technologies can be used to build on existing knowledge and to develop new epistemologies or strengthen old ones. (p. 1029)

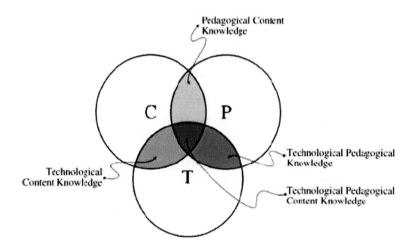

Figure 2: Technological Pedagogical Content Knowledge Framework
(from Mishra & Koehler, 2006)

Results from our studies confirm that building a community of inquiry in the 21st century classroom cannot be accomplished with educational technology alone. Even if teachers and students possess, to varying degrees, technology knowledge about software and hardware, they must be attentive to how learning in the discipline might be improved by "complex relationships between technology, content, and pedagogy, and [by] using this understanding to develop appropriate, context-specific strategies and representations" (Mishra & Koehler, 2006, p. 1029). In other words, using technology in educational design cannot be understood simply as an add-on component to established course work. It must lead to a fundamental reconsideration of disciplinary content knowledge and pedagogy so as to develop a coherent educational framework that recognizes how teaching and learning can be changed as a result of technological affordances.

In history education, such understanding can take the form of technology-designed-based lessons and units structured around active learning and doing of digital history that transcends traditional roles of "transmitter" and "receiver." By having technological affordances directly in the classroom, both students and teachers can partake in learning activities that ultimately change the nature of learning due to the pedagogical tools at their disposal. Perhaps more importantly, teaching through this approach allows for classroom-situated learning with technology, that is, a nuanced understanding of how specific educational technology applies, or not, to particular classrooms and teachers. In the case of the VH, for example, a technology-designed based activity on the October Crisis could involve a combination of teacher- and student-centred lessons on historical inquiry. Using such tools as a smartboard and the VH program, the teacher could explicitly teach students how to search and read historical documents (e.g., Cabinet conclusions) using a set of heuristics embedded in the program. Having mastered the intellectual process of historical reading, students can then be put into small groups to engage in additional sourcing with material provided by the Virtual library. As a culminating task, they could – individually or in groups – use the VH program to create their own historical interpretations. The role of the teacher would inevitably shift from "lecturer" to "coach" (Gaffield, 2002), providing support as students employ disciplinary thinking tools to read, analyze, compare, and develop meaning from the sources.

Technology in education is inevitable. Yet no single technology can apply universally to teachers. Teaching, as Shulman (1986) established, is a complex activity that cannot be reduced to a set of pedagogical steps that invariably produce positive outcomes. Teachers must be flexible in their use of knowledge to design successful lessons adapted to their audience with the most effective learning tools at their disposal. Digital history programs, such as the Virtual Historian, provide an additional technology to achieve inquiry-based learning in history.

REFERENCES

Ashburn, E., Baildon, M., Damico, J., & McNair, S. (2006). Mapping the terrain for meaningful learning using technology in social studies. In E. Ashburn & R. Floden (Eds.), *Meaningful learning using technology: What educators need to know and do* (pp. 117–140). New York: Teachers College Press.

Bain, R. (2006). Seeing the meaning "hidden" in history and social studies teaching. In E. Ahsburn & R. Floden (Eds.), *Meaningful learning using technology: What educators need to know and do* (pp. 87–116). New York: Teachers College Press.

Britt, A., Perfetti, C., Van Dyke, J., & Gabrys, G. (2000). The sourcer's apprentice: A tool for document-supported instruction. In P. Stearns, P. Seixas, & S. Wineburg (Eds.), *Knowing, teaching and learning history: National and international perspectives* (pp. 437–470). New York: New York University Press.

Bussières, P., & Gluszynski T. (2002). *The impact of computer use on reading achievement of 15-year-olds.* Paper presented at PERC Symposium, Montreal, Quebec, Canada. Retrieved February 1, 2007, from http://www-pisa.gc.ca/SP-599-05-04E.pdf

Cohen, D., & Rosenzweig, R. (2005). *Digital history: A guide to gathering, preserving, and presenting the past on the web.* Philadelphia: University of Pennsylvania Press. Retrieved from http://chnm.gmu.edu/digitalhistory

DeWitt, S. (2007). Dividing the digital divide: Instructional use of computers in social studies. *Theory and Research in Social Education, 35*(2), 277–304.

Dunning, P. (2001, Fall). From the editor. *Education Canada.* Retrieved April 19, 2008, from http://www.cea-ace.ca/pub.cfm?subsection=edu&page=arc&subpage=fal01

Friedman, A. (2006). World history teachers' use of digital primary sources: The effect of training. *Theory and Research in Social Education, 34*(1), 124–141.

Gaffield, C. (2002, October). Toward the coach in the history classroom. *Canadian Issues,* 12–14.

Lee, J., & Calandra, B. (2004). Can embedded annotations help high school students perform problem solving tasks using a web-based historical document? *Journal of Research on Technology in Education, 36*(4), 65–84.

Lévesque, S. (2006, Fall). Learning by "playing": Engaging students in digital history. *Canadian Issues,* 68–71.

Levstik, L., & Barton, K. (2001). *Doing history: Investigating with children in elementary and middle Schools* (2nd ed.). Mahwah, NJ: Lawrence Erlbaum.

Milson, A. (2002). The internet and inquiry learning: Integrating medium and method in a sixth grade social studies classroom. *Theory and Research in Social Education, 30*(3), 330–353.

Mishra, P., & Koehler, M. (2006). Technological pedagogical content knowledge: A framework for teacher knowledge. *Teachers College Record, 108*(6), 1017–1054.

Ontario Ministry of Education. (2005). *Canadian and world studies, grades 9-10 – Revised.* Toronto, ON: Queen's Printer.

Pan, B., Hembrooke, H., Joachims, T., Lorigo, L., Gay, G., & Granka, L. (2007). In Google we trust: Users' decisions on rank, position, and relevance. *Journal of Computer-Mediated Communication, 12,* 801–823.

Sandwell, R. (2005). "Who killed William Robinson"? Exploring a nineteenth-century murder online. *Social Education, 68*(3), 210–213.

Saye, J., & Brush, T. (2004). Scaffolding problem-based teaching in a traditional social studies classroom. *Theory and Research in Social Education, 32*(3), 349–378.

Saye, J., & Brush, T. (2006a). Comparing teachers' strategies for supporting student inquiry in a problem-based multimedia-enhanced history unit. *Theory and Research in Social Education, 34*(2), 183–212.

Saye, J., & Brush, T. (2006b, April). *Scaffolding critical reasoning in history and social studies: Tools to support problem-based historical inquiry.* Paper presented at the Annual meeting of the American Educational Research Association, San Francisco, CA.

Saye, J., & Brush, T. (2007). Using technology-enhanced learning environments to support problem-based historical inquiry in secondary school classrooms. *Theory and Research in Social Education, 35*(2), 196–230.

Seixas, P. (1993). The community of inquiry as a basis for knowledge and learning: The case of history. *American Educational Research Journal, 30*(2), 305–324.

Seixas, P. (2002). The purposes of teaching Canadian history. *Canadian Social Studies, 36*(2). Retrieved April 1, 2008, from http://www.quasar.ualberta.ca/css/Css_36_2/ARpurposes_teaching_canadian_history.htm

Shemilt, D. (1987). Adolescent ideas about evidence and methodology. In C. Portal (Ed.), *The history curriculum for teachers* (pp. 39–61). London: Falmer Press.

Shulman, L. (1986). Those who understand: Knowledge growth in teaching. *Educational Researcher, 15*(2), 4–14.

Swan, K. O., & Hofer, M. (2008). Technology and social studies. In L. Levstik & C. Tyson (Eds.), *Handbook of research in social studies education* (pp. 207–236). New York: Routledge.

Tally, B. (2007). Digital technology and the end of social studies education. *Theory and Research in Social Education, 35*(2), 305–321.

VanSledright, B. (2002). *In search of America's past: Learning to read history in elementary school.* New York: Teachers College Press.

VanSledright, B. (2004). What does it means to think historically... and how do you teach it? *Social Education, 68*(3), 230–233.

Virtual Historian. (n.d.). *The virtual historian.* Retrieved April 1, 2008, from http://www.virtualhistorian.ca/

Voss, J., & Wiley, J. (2000). A case study of developing historical understanding via instruction. In P. Stearns, P. Seixas, & S. Wineburg (Eds.), *Knowing, teaching and learning history: National and international perspectives* (pp. 375–389). New York: New York University Press.

Wiggins, G., & McTighe, J. (2005). *Understanding by design* (2nd ed.). Alexandria, VA: Association for Supervision and Curriculum Development.

Wineburg, S. (2001). *Historical thinking and other unnatural acts: Charting the future of teaching the past.* Philadelphia: Temple University Press.

Yeager, E. A., & Doppen F. H. (2001). Teaching and learning multiple perspectives on the use of the atomic bomb: Historical empathy in the secondary classroom. In O. L. Davis, A. Yeager, & S. Foster (Eds.), *Historical empathy and perspective taking in the social studies* (pp. 97–114). Lanham, MD: Rowman & Littlefield.

Stéphane Lévesque
University of Ottawa
Canada

3. RE-PRESENTING CANADIAN HISTORY ON-LINE

"The Cyberterrorism Crisis" Web Site as a Test Case of History and Citizenship Education on the Web

INTRODUCTION

Following the terrorist attacks of September 11, 2001, governments around the world took measures to increase their security in an effort to prevent future strikes. In Canada, the federal government passed Bill C-36, The Anti-Terrorism Act, to bolster the powers of law-enforcement and security agencies. According to the prime minister and his minister of justice, the new bill appropriately expanded government power without trampling on fundamental freedoms. Critics of the legislation, however, argued that this increase in the powers of the state came at the expense of Canadians' civil liberties. They pointed to what they saw as disquieting parallels between the new legislation and the War Measures Act of the past.[1] During World War I, World War II, and the 1970 October Crisis, the War Measures Act had been used by law-enforcement agencies to arrest and detain innocent people. As the government moved to increase security, was it repeating past mistakes or taking necessary precautions in the face of a legitimate threat?

Since the autumn of 2001, concerned Canadian citizens have grappled with this question. The October 12, 2002 nightclub bombings in Bali, Indonesia, which killed 202 men and women, the March 11, 2004, train bombings in Madrid, which resulted in 200 deaths, and the July 7, 2005, subway and bus bombings in London, which killed fifty-two people, testify to a continuing threat. The September 18, 2006 report of Justice Denis O'Connor into the rendition and torture in a Syrian jail of Canadian citizen Maher Arar bears witness to the need to protect personal liberties. How then, should our government balance the need to safeguard the freedom of individuals with the need to maintain the security of all?

For many high school teachers this is a "teachable moment": those leading social studies and civics classes have an opportunity to elucidate contemporary dilemmas by situating these in historical context; those leading history classes have the chance to illustrate how lessons drawn from the study of the past might provide insight into the present. For all teachers interested in engaging students in deliberations of contemporary issues, discussions concerning the roles of citizens in a democratic society are no longer "academic." But what should teachers tell their students about the debate? More specifically, how should educators frame the liberty-security debate for students? And how might knowledge of the history of the War Measures Act facilitate or impede an understanding of the present challenge? Finally, what tools could best aid educators teaching young people about the past and the debate in the present?

T. Di Petta (Ed.), The Emperor's New Computer: ICT, Teachers and Teaching, 29–44.
© 2008 Sense Publishers. All rights reserved.

In the months prior to September 11, 2001, my team and I had begun production of a bilingual Web site focused on the War Measures Act at the National Film Board of Canada (NFB). The issues addressed in the site became increasingly relevant following the terrorist attacks, and we focused our efforts toward the production of an educational tool that would meet the needs of high school teachers addressing the liberty-security debate with their students in the context of Canadian history.[2] Drawing on the insights of educational researchers, this paper outlines the theoretical framework that guided our work, as well as the decisions that we made to: (a) adopt a structure that promoted discussion while reminding students that points-of-view are grounded in life experience; (b) use history, with its potentially contradictory lessons, as a reference point to understand the present; and (c) draw on the properties of the World Wide Web to facilitate student understanding of the contemporary debate and the lessons of history concerning that debate.

The teaching of citizenship and history in Canadian schools has been the subject of considerable discussion in recent years; so too has been the use of new technologies. This paper attempts to contribute to those discussions by highlighting some of the lessons drawn from the production of one new media tool. In this way, the project, which came to be called "The Cyber-Terrorism Crisis," serves as one test case of doing history and citizenship education today on the World Wide Web. And what conclusions may be derived from this test-case? In the pages that follow, I will outline how Web simulations can be especially effective for facilitating student understanding of the complex nature of contemporary issues, such as those concerning the balancing of liberty and security in post-9/11 Canada.

DEBATE FRAMEWORK: THE PUBLIC ISSUES AND ALTERNATIVE MODELS

Several weeks following September 11, 2001, *Social Education*, the official journal of the National Council for the Social Studies (in the United States) published a special section describing strategies for educating students about the fallout of the attacks. In an article promoting classroom discussion and reflection on public issues in a time of crisis, author Laurel Singleton (2001) pointed out that "Democracy requires the expression of differing opinions and the examination of alternative perspectives in the belief that the truth is most likely to emerge following candid discussions of all dimensions of an issue" (p. 413). To guide discussions surrounding questions such as "To what extent, if any, should U.S. citizens' rights be abridged in order to improve security?" Singleton encouraged teachers to follow the Public Issues Model (p. 416).[3]

With roots in the Harvard Social Studies Project, which experimented with a social studies curriculum based on analysis of public controversy (see Levin, Newmann, & Oliver, 1969; Oliver & Shaver, 1966), the Public Issues Model was developed in the 1960s and promoted in the United States and Canada (see Levin, 1969). Identifying a "public issue" as involving a decision around which there was disagreement, the model was based on the assumption that citizens frequently share differing opinions on important ethical or value questions, and that these opinions often conflict. The resolution of complex public issues within a democratic society therefore required citizens to negotiate their differences through careful analysis and public discussion.

In an era defined by the American civil rights movement, the rebirth of the feminist movement and, in Canada, the reassertion of nationalism in Québec, and at a time when a problem-centered approach to teaching was dominant in social studies curricula, the model was promoted as a means to teach students how to resolve ethical-moral and legal dilemmas. Recognizing that debates of this nature frequently revolved around determining which of two conflicting goods (such as liberty and security) should take priority, the model encouraged students to find solutions that compromised to the least extent the opposing values.

In the Spring of 2008, Singleton's article continued to be linked to the "Teachable Moments" Web page of the "National Council for Social Studies" Web site, and the Public Issues Model was being advocated by influential organizations such as the American "National Clearinghouse for English Language Acquisition and Language Instruction Educational Programs," which recommended the model to teachers leading discussions on "American Perspectives."[4] Armed with a clear outline of how to guide a debate, and backed by first-rate, albeit dated, research, teachers may feel adequately prepared to lead successful debates using the Public Issues Model. Yet others may find that the framework for discussion lacks a key ingredient: explicit recognition that students' opinions are partly grounded in their personal experience. Advocates of the Public Issues Model do not appear to have sufficiently accounted for those students who might be incapable of divorcing themselves from their lived experience and therefore unable to consider public issue questions "objectively." Nor do they appear to have taken into account that students might arrive to such a debate from cultural backgrounds so fundamentally different that they lack a common set of terms – a language – by which to conduct the debate. The model seems to presume, for example, that a young Saudi-Canadian can engage objectively in a debate with an Anglo-Canadian concerning the merits of racial profiling of Arabs by the Royal Canadian Mounted Police (RCMP). In this way the Public Issues Model, while ground-breaking in its time, is hampered by the environment of ideological liberalism out of which it has emerged. It does not take sufficient account of how present-day viewpoints are connected to identity and experiences of justice. As a result, the model seems to be ill-equipped to meet the needs of teachers of 21st century multi-ethnic classes.

Present-day educators working in heterogeneous societies, such as Ulster history teacher Ben Walsh, advocate a different approach – one that begins by acknowledging that a student arrives to a public issue discussion with a viewpoint grounded in her life experience. From her riverbank of self-knowledge she surveys the public issue stream and the various and contradictory arguments that lay scattered through it. Any attempt to move the student to the riverbank on the other side of the stream, to a different understanding of the issue, must provide secure stepping stones. If these are to be useful they must look somewhat familiar – they must be close to her riverbank of understanding. Secure in her self-knowledge, she will have the confidence to venture onto stepping stones of differing opinions and give consideration to arguments that challenge her own. In the absence of these stepping stones, the student will not reach the other side and will not gain a true understanding of the issue. And without that knowledge, she will be incapable of working with her peers to find a resolution to the problem.[5]

Promoting these kinds of experiences, in which students recognize and even value differences, is increasingly viewed as a central tenet of contemporary citizenship education. Some critics of this approach have argued that good citizenship education emphasizes what Canadians have in common (Granatstein, 1998), and few would disagree with this notion. Yet questions concerning the best response to the potential of future terrorist attacks are inherently divisive, and those who facilitate discussion of these questions must recognize that common bonds of community can quickly disintegrate in the face of such an issue. What is required of citizens in these situations, and incumbent on citizenship education in secondary schools, is that students are sensitive to the different viewpoints and life experiences of their peers.

This kind of citizenship education is especially important in our multicultural age, in which schools are composed of students from a multitude of different language groups. As philosopher Charles Taylor has observed, 21st century culture is marked by globalization and a tremendous rise in international migration and the consequent diversification of the population. Adding to the dissolution of a common identity is increasing differentiation within the population. As a result of the feminist and other movements, unity on political issues has faded, replaced by an increased diversity of opinion. We are witnessing the rise of what Taylor has called a "diasporic consciousness." According to Taylor (1998), "People now live in imagined spaces, spaces where they see themselves situated within a certain society and more and more of these spaces straddle borders and other boundaries" (p. 332). As a result, it is impossible to share a common identity, "a sort of uniform citizenship," which, "like a hockey sweater, we must all fit into in the same way." To force consensus on an increasingly multicultural society would only result in the alienation of young people, especially "recent arrivals" who "want to be part of a process whose real history is in the future, not the past" (pp. 339–340). What is needed, instead, is a citizenship that values these differences – that recognizes that such diversity makes us more dynamic in a world where we find ourselves increasingly in contact with people from other countries.[6]

Many young people would welcome this kind of citizenship – research shows that this is how they view themselves. Following a study of 2,500 young people, aged 18-25, in several countries, Université Laval historian Bogumil Jewsiewicki (1999) concluded that:

> Le défi de la mondialisation… c'est que je peux être plusieurs choses à la fois… ça veut dire qu'on peut raconter plusieurs histoires à la fois. Ce que les jeunes veulent obtenir, c'est la liberté de se sentir plus solidaires avec telle communauté imaginaire plutôt qu'avec telle autre.[7]

DEBATE CONTENT: THE LESSONS OF HISTORY

If the most effective way to *teach* student-citizens about a divisive public issue is to *engage* them in the debate in a way that encourages them to be open to and respectful of the different viewpoints of others, what content might facilitate such a discussion? In the case of the federal government's actions in the aftermath of September 11th, the content was pre-determined: Bill C-36, according to some, resembled the War Measures Act of the past. In the same way that the War Measures Act had been used to arrest and detain people who had committed no crime, so Bill C-36 might be used to target innocent Canadians.

The critics' conflation of the laws past and present seemed warranted. The War Measures Act had given Prime Minister Robert Borden and his Cabinet the authority to assume unrestricted emergency powers in times of war and "apprehended insurrection." As a result, they had been able to pass laws without accountability to Parliament or to laws that had been created previously. Specifically, the War Measures Act had given the government, through federal agents such as police or the military, the power to censor the media, arrest, detain, and deport people, and to take control over their property. In effect, the law had suspended civil rights and had given dictatorial powers to the Prime Minister and Cabinet (see Borden, 1938; Brown, 1980; Brunet, 1963; Peppin, 1993).

Similarly, The Anti-Terrorism Act gave law enforcement authorities dramatic new powers. While the law was subject to the Canadian Charter of Rights and Freedoms, thus ensuring the protection of Canadians' civil rights as defined by the Charter, it nevertheless appeared to have the potential to violate civil rights in at least two ways. First, the law gave police the power of "preventative arrest" or "arrest without warrant" – to arrest and hold people suspected of being involved in "terrorist activities"; these were left undefined and did not have to be criminal acts. Second, the bill provided for "investigative hearings." Instead of compelling people to testify at a trial, as before, suspects could be forced to provide testimony at the investigative stage. If they refused, they could be charged with contempt of court and jailed.

Critics of these aspects of the bill demanded that the government include a "sunset clause" to extinguish the law or parts of the law after a defined period of time. If Bill C-36 was meant to respond to a temporary crisis, they reasoned, the new police powers should be stripped from the bill once the crisis had passed. In the end, the federal government acquiesced: the powers would lapse on December 31, 2006.[8] At the same time, however, the government stipulated that they could be renewed by a resolution in the House of Commons and Senate. In theory, these powers could remain in effect for decades to come. Similarly, the War Measures Act, conceived as a stopgap measure to meet an immediate crisis, had remained on the books until 1988. During the 74 intervening years, the law had been used on three occasions, with devastating results for the civil rights of some who lived in Canada.

Following passage of the War Measures Act in 1914, the federal government had taken steps to limit the freedom of "enemy aliens" – unnaturalized immigrants from countries with which Canada was at war. These immigrants, many of whom were Ukrainian, and therefore citizens of Canada's enemy, Austria, had chosen to not become naturalized Canadian citizens. (Most were single men who had planned to work in Canada for a few years and then return to their country.)

As the Canadian economy had deteriorated, many of these men had lost their jobs and had moved from city to city in search of work. When Canadians had demanded that the government respond to the crisis of unemployed immigrants in their cities, the government had taken action, using the powers granted by the War Measures Act to place unemployed enemy aliens in internment camps. In total, 5, 954 "Austro-Hungarians," the majority Ukrainians, had been detained. While conditions in the internment camps had varied, everywhere prisoners' mail had been censored and their movement restricted. In some cases, the camp guards had treated the prisoners well; in other cases, the prisoners had been less fortunate (for an overview of the historiography, see Gerus & Rea, 1985, p. 10; Martynowych, 1991, pp. 323–334; Melnycky, 1983; Yasnowskyj, 1978).

A similar process had unfolded during World War II; on this occasion Japanese Canadians had suffered as a result of the use of the War Measures Act. In the months that had followed the bombing of the American naval base at Pearl Harbour, Japanese forces had scored quick victories throughout Southeast Asia. Many British Columbians had become fearful that Japan would attack their province. Rumors had circulated that Japanese spies had helped Japanese troops invade other countries in 1941 and early 1942. Would Japanese Canadians living in British Columbia aid a Japanese invasion of Canada? According to the RCMP, the Canadian army and the Canadian navy, Japanese Canadians had not been a threat to Canada. (In fact, no Japanese Canadian was ever convicted of spying.) They had been convinced that the greatest threat had come from racist British Canadians who might harm Japanese Canadians. Prime Minister King, for his part, had been concerned that attacks on people of Japanese descent living in Canada might have led Japanese soldiers to harm Canadian prisoners of war. Nevertheless, to appease public opinion Prime Minister King and his Cabinet had issued Order-in-Council P.C. No. 1486 (an amendment to the Defence of Canada Regulations created under the War Measures Act) on February 24, 1942, ordering the removal of Japanese Canadians from their homes to camps in the interior of B.C.

Altogether, 21,000 had been forced to move from their homes. Nearly 12,000 Japanese Canadians had relocated to housing camps. Others had taken jobs on sugar beet farms in Alberta, Manitoba, and Ontario. A few had joined friends and relatives, and others with money of their own had moved to interior B.C. towns where they had worked in lumbering and agriculture or lived off their savings. The forced relocation of Japanese Canadians had not been a temporary measure – the government had intended to permanently remove them from coastal B.C. In January 1943 the process had been completed: drawing on the powers of the War Measures Act, the Prime Minister and Cabinet had issued an Order-in-Council authorizing the liquidation of property belonging to Japanese Canadians. (This property had been held in trust by the government, on the understanding that it would be returned to Japanese Canadians at the end of the war.) Japanese boats, homes, and businesses had been sold, often at prices well below normal.[9]

Three decades later, the War Measures Act had been used again. At 4 am on October 16, 1970 the federal government, led by Prime Minister Pierre Trudeau, had proclaimed the law in force, suspending Canadians' liberties during the October Crisis. The Crisis had begun when two men had kidnapped James Cross, the British Trade Commissioner, in Montréal. Later that day, a ransom note had identified the kidnappers as members of the Libération cell of the Front de Libération du Québec (FLQ); they had threatened to execute Cross if their demands were not met. The crisis had escalated on October 10, when Pierre Laporte, the Québec Minister of Labour and Manpower and Minister of Immigration, had been kidnapped from his home by two masked men from another cell of the FLQ. Following Laporte's kidnapping, many Canadians had feared a wide-spread terrorist conspiracy.

Prime Minister Trudeau and Justice Minister John Turner had argued that use of the War Measures Act was necessary given the "erosion of the public will" and the "state of confusion that existed in the province of Québec" (Boulanger, 2004). The government had already used available powers to call out the army. Now further action was needed. Public Order Regulations passed under the Act had declared the FLQ an "unlawful organisation," and had made membership in the FLQ punishable by up to 5 years in prison. Attending a meeting of an unlawful association or speaking publicly in advocacy of one had become cause for suspicion. The Public Order regulations had also provided for seizure of property without a warrant, arrest without a warrant, and detention of prisoners without bail, without charge for 21 days and without trial for up to 90 days. In the 48 hours that had followed the invoking of the War Measures Act, the Montréal city police and the Québec provincial police had used the extraordinary powers that they had been given to arrest 250 people in Québec. Among those detained were members of the Parti Québécois, labor leaders, poets, singers, and journalists. Many had connections to the Québec independence movement; very few had committed a crime.

Suspects had been placed in often over-crowded prison cells and had been questioned repeatedly by police. Some of the prisoners had later alleged that they had been beaten in the course of these interrogations. The detainees had not been allowed to contact their families or a lawyer (they were finally given access to legal counsel on October 26) – in many cases, their families had had no idea where they were. Most had been released after spending seven days in prison, though some had been held considerably longer. In the end, of the 465 people arrested under the powers granted by the War Measures Act, 403 had been released without charge, and 18 had been found guilty of a crime.[10]

In three crisis environments, World War I, World War II, and the October Crisis, sweeping legislation had been put into effect allowing for the arrest and detainment of people who had done nothing wrong. Would history be repeated? As the federal government attempted in the autumn of 2001 to respond to the threat of future terrorist attacks, it appeared that its efforts to ensure the security of the country might once again infringe on Canadians' civil liberties. For some critics, the pattern was clear: in the creation and application of Bill C-36, the federal government would be repeating the mistakes of the War Measures Act. Minority Canadians – in this case Arab Canadians – might be targeted and perhaps mistreated.

Seven years later, we know that while mass arrests are indeed "history," the mistakes of the past have been repeated. Maher Arar, a Canadian citizen of Syrian origin, was identified in a May 2002 presentation by the RCMP to American authorities as a candidate for a Bill C-36 "investigative hearing." Detained a few months later by American officials on suspicion of terrorism, Arar was eventually sent to Syria where he was repeatedly tortured. Innocent of all charges, he was released a year later.[11] The House of Commons and the Commissioner of the RCMP apologized for his detention and torture, but for Arar, this is of little comfort.

Several years after the introduction of Bill C-36, we can see clear parallels between events of the past and present; but the lessons of history are murky. In the present context, it may be argued that Bill C-36 has helped the government prevent terrorist attacks. Looking back to the past, it might be pointed out that while internment suspended the liberties of Ukrainians, it also provided food and shelter to destitute citizens of an enemy country. No Japanese Canadian had been convicted of spying against Canada, but some hardliners who had openly expressed their loyalty to Japan might have committed espionage if not for internment (Granatstein & Johnson, 1988). Was it not possible, as Pierre Trudeau argued later, that the swift actions of his government in 1970 were responsible for putting an end to violent protest in Québec, and ensuring peace in the years that followed? Perhaps, in suspending the liberties of some, the government had ensured the security of all. How could the past shed light on the present if previous situations had ended without an historical consensus – if the verdict of history had been rendered by a hung jury?

Influential commentators have argued that history, as a central component of secondary school citizenship education, should be taught as one story, building a base of common knowledge among young Canadians (Fowler, 1995; Granatstein, 1988, pp. 21–50; McLeod, 1982). Few would question the value of understanding the events and championing the people that have made Canada one of the most envied countries on the planet. But it cannot end there because teaching history in this manner proves insufficient at exactly the moment when an understanding of history is especially important: when groups make claims of the past to support their political agendas in the present. Does the past provide lessons to help us determine if Bill C-36 is a wise response to the present crisis? In this situation, there is no single answer.[12] As educator Peter Lee (1998) notes, "The past can not ... be plundered to prove any case or to make any contemporary social or moral point.... because the past is complex and does not sanctify any particular social or personal position above another" (p. 53).

Some critics of the contemporary teaching of history in high schools have argued that the inclusion of social history has diluted the story of Canada's past to the point that it is meaningless to young people. According to these critics, history at this level should instead give priority to the evolution of the Canadian nation-state.[13] Yet in the case of the War Measures Act, an analysis of political events tells only one side of the story. The work of social historians has provided considerable insight into how the actions of the government, specifically its use of provisions of the law, affected groups such as Ukrainians, Japanese Canadians, and French-Canadian nationalists. In the process, historian A. B. McKillop (1999) has observed, the insights of social historians have provided us with knowledge of the failures, not just the successes of the past; they have given us accounts of the weak and anonymous to supplement the chronicles of the strong and celebrated.

These critics of high school history have also lamented the emphasis on "process" and specifically students' examination of conflicting historical interpretations (Granatstein, 1998). A pedagogy that gives attention to the way in which history might be told from different perspectives, using different kinds of evidence, is altogether too complicated for a fifteen-year-old, say the critics. As Peter Lee (1998) points out, this is a strange criticism because

> it is clear that this is true as much for teaching one account as for teaching the nature of the discipline. Why should it be a problem that students' ideas about historians' accounts are immature and partially developed, but not a problem that their ideas about (say) the French Revolution, or women's role in politics since 1918, are in the same state? (p. 53)

Furthermore, how are students to understand the sometimes contradictory conclusions of historians if they do not know how these judgments were constructed?

Research indicates that secondary school students are cognitively ready to begin to deal with the complexities of different historical interpretations. A study conducted by Peter Lee and Rosalyn Ashby (2000) led them to conclude that, while second and fifth grade students had difficulty explaining the existence of

> two different stories about the same bit of history.... a small proportion of mainly sixth- and eighth- grade students showed signs of understanding that it was in the nature of historical accounts to differ. They recognized that accounts could not be complete and had to fit parameters.... In the sixth and eighth grades... students began to explain differences by pointing out that evidence needs interpretation. (p. 210)

This kind of understanding must be a central component of a citizenship education for secondary school students who will be eligible, soon after graduation, to vote, serve on juries, and decide for themselves the proper balance between liberty and security.

DEBATE TOOL: THE CYBER-TERRORISM CRISIS WEB SITE

In the case of the history of the War Measures Act, it is only through the study of social history as well as political history, and only through an understanding of the process of writing history, (for instance the choice of which of the voices of the past are given priority) that students can *begin* to understand the past, and draw on that understanding to better understand the dilemmas of the present. But if history provides parallels to the Anti-Terrorism Act, but no clear verdict on how to best safeguard civil liberties while ensuring the security of society, what kind of educational tool might assist an exploration of the nuances of the debate? In the space that remains, I will outline how the kinds of learning processes that lead to effective discussions concerning public issues may be facilitated by sites such as The Cyber-Terrorism Crisis.

The last several years have witnessed the emergence of a plethora of digital teaching tools. Many of these have taken advantage of the encyclopedic powers of digital technologies to produce libraries and archives of electronic texts, providing students with access to data and documents previously available only with great difficulty and expense. While these resources have made significant contributions to improving the study of history and citizenship, there are other ways in which these might be employed to educate young people.

We are only beginning to learn how to effectively use the new computer technologies. These are in a cradle stage of development, a period of technical evolution. As a result, we are still struggling to define the conventions of coherent communication appropriate to them. And what at first appear to be digital technology's liabilities may, in the future, be considered its greatest strengths. For instance, many criticize the Web because it seems to encourage restlessness and promote shortened attention spans (as reflected in the term "Web surfing"). Yet it may be argued that by providing access to information previously unavailable, the Web encourages students to embark on their own journeys of discovery. "Perhaps," as David Weinberger (2002) has observed, "the Web isn't shortening our attention span. Perhaps the world is just getting more interesting" (p. 69).

"Perhaps too interesting," some teachers might reply. Sending students onto the Web without a clear task can bring dreadful results; Web sites often work best when they serve as one component of a curriculum unit. For this reason my team and I created a "Teachers' Centre" so that "The Cyber-Terrorism Crisis" could be integrated into teachers' larger goals for their history, civics, or social studies classes.[14] Only with the guidance of his or her teacher, we were convinced, could a student charting a course through a Web site be an active learner, examining different pieces of content in the quest for knowledge.[15]

In situations such as this, the student decides which path to follow, but she does not necessarily know where her journey will take her. This may be one of the most exciting qualities of the technology: its capacity to surprise. The Web, with its links enabling one document to be connected to another, creates environments in which associations can be made between people, events, and ideas, across time and space. As a medium, notes Weinberger (2002), "the Web is built thoroughly and completely out of the interrelationship of things" (p. 170). Sometimes those associations are obvious; on other occasions they are unforeseen.

In her seminal work on narrative and digital media, Victorian literature scholar and educational software designer Janet Murray has described the aesthetics of digital technologies as: (a) immersion – the sense of being surrounded by another reality; (b) agency – the ability to do things for which we can see tangible results; and (c) transformation – the ability to explore process, to capture experience as systems of interrelated actions. The properties of the technology, in this case the student's ability to become immersed in the world of the Web and to act as an independent agent as she explores a collection of documents, allows her to rotate her point of view, capturing both shared reality and separate experience. As a result, her understanding of a narrative can change shape and transform. She has the potential to see things from a different point of view – one of an educator's central goals for public issues discussions.

This potential allows for exciting ways to, in this case, discover what happened in the past, and the different meanings of those events. Murray (1997) suggests, for example, that "The format that most fully exploits the properties of digital environments is... the simulation: the virtual world full of interrelated entities, a world we can enter, manipulate, and observe in process" (p. 280). Applied to a public issues question, in which a student would be confronted with evidence that challenges his viewpoint, a Web site simulation could allow him to work through the problem in a virtual world.

Student learning may have improved because the simulations and applications required the students to "do something" with the knowledge that they had acquired. The conclusions of the recent "cognitive revolution" in psychology are unequivocal: learning is significantly enhanced when students go beyond mental representations and instead solve problems – when they put their learning into action. As Howard Gardner (1998), one of the leaders of the cognitive revolution, has put it,

> Understanding will never come about through the piling of facts. It can only emerge if students have the opportunity to tackle authentic problems; to use their skills appropriately in plausible settings; to create projects, alone and in cooperation; to receive feedback on these endeavors and ultimately to become willing productive thinkers. (p. viii)

Beginning in the autumn of 2001, the "problem" of balancing liberty and security in a time of crisis was all too "authentic." The historical analogies to the War Measures Act were also "authentic": references to the law appeared frequently in the media. What was needed, then, was a computer-based simulation that could serve as an effective learning tool, engaging students in a debate where they could be both secure in their own viewpoint and open to contrasting interpretations, providing them with the opportunity to examine historical events from a variety of perspectives. This was our goal as we created "The Cyber-Terrorism Crisis" Web site.

The site began with a fictitious scenario that echoed (rather than mirrored) the events of September 11, 2001: a group of cyber-terrorists had shut down major computer databases, resulting in considerable damage. The Prime Minister had suggested that the government invoke emergency legislation – in this case, the Emergencies Act, which had replaced the War Measures Act in 1988. The Emergencies Act had never been used, but appeared to have the potential to infringe on civil liberties. Students were ultimately asked to vote, as Canadian citizens, in an online referendum, for or against the use of the law. At the heart of the dilemma was a choice between safeguarding individual liberties and championing collective security. This was the narrative framework – the painting that we placed upon the canvas.

Students had several options within this narrative framework, and thus the opportunity to experience the story – the painting on the canvas – in different ways.

To facilitate their decision, they were given the chance to travel back in time and encounter characters – Prime Ministers, Canadians who supported them, and prisoners – who had experienced similar events during World War I, World War II, and the October Crisis. From these characters the students heard contrasting viewpoints on the legitimacy of the government's use of the law. For example, Prime Minister King recalled his concern for the safety of Japanese Canadians living in British Columbia, while a young woman in an internment camp observed that she had been removed from her home though she had done nothing wrong. In addition, summaries of the events were provided to offer context. And students were given the opportunity, through online forums, to engage in discussion with their peers regarding the choice between liberty and security in the past and present. In the end they had to vote for or against the government's use of the Emergencies Act. But between entering the site and leaving, students were free to explore the content as they wished. They might have opted to give priority to evidence or viewpoints that supported their own. At some point, however, they would have encountered the counter-argument. Students who had entered the site convinced that security was the first priority might have changed their minds when confronted by the testimony of those who had lost their civil liberties, and then their freedom. Others who had initially sympathized with the victims might have been persuaded that the potential infringement of the rights of a few might sometimes be necessary to maintain the security of the many.

In our simulation, students were placed in front of a kaleidoscopic canvas that captured events from different perspectives. They recognized that there was no single reality, no single integrating view of the world, no single angle of perception. The site provided multiple views of the past and present, while at the same time honoring a desire to fix reality on one canvas by tying the events together in an integrated manner. The story was complex and multifaceted, yet still coherent. And the lessons were not altogether clear. Students learned that the past, like the present, does not render simple judgments.

CONCLUSION

The site has succeeded on various levels. Students have encountered the difficulty in finding a balance between the liberty of the individual and the security of the collective in times of crisis. Many of them have understood that the effects of legislation such as The Anti-Terrorism Act cannot be easily predicted. Many have developed empathy for marginalized groups, such as the Japanese Canadians during World War II. Those who have written essays about their experience of the site have recognized that their understanding of the story, and their vote, might have changed if they had listened to different viewpoints from the past and considered different evidence.

The process of production of the Web site has provided some insight into the effective use of Web simulations to teach history and citizenship to secondary school students. Educators designing tools to facilitate public debates need to take into account the contemporary reality that students come to these discussions with viewpoints grounded in their different life experiences. Yet their understanding of contemporary public issues is far from static and can change as they learn about a history that is multiple in its perspectives and ambiguous in its conclusions.

Finally, new computer technologies provide exciting opportunities to teach the multiplicity of historical understandings in novel and effective ways. As these technologies evolve, educators will continue to exploit their potential for the study of history and civics. In his book, *What Video Games Have to Teach Us About Learning and Literacy*, James Paul Gee (2003) points out that computer games are especially good at enabling players to explore new worlds (including those in the past), and develop resources for problem solving. Just as we are using the Web today, so educators of the future may employ simulations, games, and other emerging technologies to engage students in the study of the past, so that they may better understand, if not resolve, the challenges of the present.

NOTES

[1] In Montréal, to cite just one example, concerned citizens met at "Conférence: C-36, nouvelle Loi des measures de guerre?" on December 12, 2001. Questions addressed at the conference included: "La repression à grande échelle est-elle une chose du passé? Sommes-nous maintenant à l'abri d'une telle violence du pouvoir politique?" The answer was clear to the conference organizers: "Au moment où le gouvernement fédéral s'apprête à adopter le projet de loi antiterroriste C-36, nous pouvons certainement en douter." Invited speakers included Serge Mongeau, author of Kidnappé par la Police, which described his incarceration during the 1970 October Crisis.

[2] The Web site, a production of the English and French Programs at the National Film Board of Canada, was released under the title "The Cyber-Terrorism Crisis" in May 2002 (http://www.nfb.ca/ enclasse/wma/ [Retrieved May 8, 2008]) and subsequently won Honorable Mention at the 2002 International New Media Awards. I was the Director of the project, Marie-Jacques Rouleau was the Designer, and Chantal Ide the Developer. The Producer was Michael Fukushima, and David Verrall and Marcel Jean were the Executive Producers.

[3] Singleton's article is based, in part, on: L. R. Singleton and J. R. Griese's Preparing citizens to participate in democratic discourse: The public issues model (2007). In R. Evans and David Saxe, (Eds।), Handbook on teaching social issues: NCSS bulletin 93 (pp. 59-65).Washington, DC: National Council for the Social Studies.

[4] The "Teachable Moments" Web page of the "National Council for Social Studies" Web site may be found at http://www.socialstudies.org/resources/moments/ [Retrieved May 8, 2008]; Singleton's article is linked to the above page, and may be found at http://downloads.ncss.org/lessons/ 650703.shtml [Retrieved May 8, 2008]. The "National Clearinghouse for English Language Acquisition and Language Instruction Educational Programs" Web site may be found at http://www.ncela.gwu.edu/ [Retrieved May 8, 2008]; the "Discuss American Perspectives" Web page may be found at: http://www.ncela.gwu.edu/practice/tolerance/1_perspectives.htm [Retrieved May 8, 2008]; the "Adaptations to the Public Issues Model" Web page may be found at http://www.ncela.gwu.edu/practice/tolerance/pimodel.htm [Retrieved May 8, 2008].

[5] See the strategies that Walsh (2000) employs in his secondary school history text, The struggle for peace in Northern Ireland: A modern world study. London: John Murray Publishers.

[6] François Audigier has articulated a similar vision for citizenship education in Europe. According to Audigier: "L'identité de chacun se pense de façon plurielle. Tout homme appartient à plusieurs groupes et se définit dans ces relations de pluriappartenance. La hiérarchisation entre les différents niveaux et les différentes formes d'appartenance ne s'impose pas d'elle-même... Nous ne vivons plus

dans des sociétés où l'identité collective puisse se pense de façon homogène, c'est-à-dire où se recouvrent un groupe, un territoire, une langue, voire une religion, une économie. " Audigier, F. (1995, avril). Enseigner l'Europe: Quelques questions à l'histoire et à la géographie scolaires. Recherche et Formation, 18, 41-42.

[7]   Le Devoir, 24 mars 1999. Jewsiewicki conducted the study with Jocelyn Letourneau, directeur du Centre d'études interdisciplinaires sur les lettres, les arts et les traditions, Université Laval. See also Bogumil Jewsiewicki et Jocelyn Létourneau, avec la collaboration de Irène Herrmann, Les jeunes à l'ère de la mondialisation. Quête identitaire et conscience historique (Sillery: Septentrion, 1998) and Bogumil Jewsiewicki et Jocelyn Létourneau, Identités en mutation, socialités en germination (Sillery: Septentrion, 1998).

[8]   These provisions subsequently expired when a government motion to renew them failed in the House of Commons in 2007.

[9]   Some of the key works on this subject include Peppin, "Emergency Legislation and Rights in Canada: The War Measures Act and Civil Liberties," 156-176; Forrest E. La Violette, The Canadian Japanese and World War II (Toronto: University of Toronto Press, 1948); J.L. Granatstein and G.A. Johnson, "The Evacuation of the Japanese Canadians, 1942: A Realist Critique of the Received Version," in Normal Hillmer et al, eds., On Guard for Thee: War, Ethnicity and the Canadian State, 1939-1945 (Ottawa: Canadian Committee for the History of the Second World War, 1988); Ken Adachi, The Enemy That Never Was (Toronto: McClelland and Stewart, 1976); Muriel Kitagawa, This is My Own: Letters to Wes and other Writings of Japanese Canadians 1941-1948 (Vancouver: Talonbooks, 1985); Brian Nolan, King's War: Mackenzie King and the Politics of War, 1939-1945 (Toronto: Fawcett Crest, 1988), 65-73; Keibo Oiwa, Stone Voices: Wartime Writings of Japanese Canadian Issei (Montréal: Véhicule Press, 1991), 115-154; Patricia Roy, J.L. Granatstein, Masako Iino, Hiroko Takamura, Mutual Hostages: Canadians and Japanese during the Second World War (Toronto: University of Toronto Press, 1990), 75-138; Ann Gomer Sunahara, The Politics of Racism: The Uprooting of Japanese Canadians During the Second World War (Toronto: Lorimer, 1981).

[10] A short bibliography on the October Crisis would include: Peppin, "Emergency Legislation and Rights in Canada: The War Measures Act and Civil Liberties," 177-189; Jean-François Duchaîne, Rapport sur les événements d'octobre 1970 (Québec: Gouvernement du Québec, 1981); Reg Whitaker, "Apprehended Insurrection? RCMP Intelligence and the October Crisis," Queen's Quarterly 100:2 (Summer 1993); Denis Smith, Bleeding Hearts, Bleeding Country: Canada and the Quebec Crisis (Edmonton: Hurtig, 1971); John F. Conway, Des comptes à rendre (Montréal: VLB Éditeur, 1995); Serge Mongeau, Kidnappé par la police (Montréal: Editions du jour, 1970); Germain Dion, Une Tournade de 60 jours: La crise d'octobre 1970 à la chambre des communes (Hull: Éditions Asticou, 1985); Claude Pelletier, Crise d'octobre: dossier de presse (Sherbrooke: Bibliothèque du Séminaire de Sherbrooke, 1988); James Stewart, The FLQ: Seven Years of Terrorism (Toronto: Simon & Schuster, 1970); House of Commons Debates (October 16, 1970), 193-246; (October 22, 1970), 451-506; (Octobre 28, 1970), 656; (October 29, 1970), 687-689; (November 2, 1970), 776-777; (November 4, 1970), 870-872; (November 4, 1970), 878-899; (November 5, 1970), 905; (November 9, 1970), 993; (November 12, 1970), 1089.

[11] Commission of Inquiry into the Actions of Canadian Officials in Relation to Maher Arar, Report of the Events Relating to Maher Arar: Analysis and Recommendations (Ottawa: Publishing and Depository Services, Public Works and Government Services Canada, 2006), 126. See also Commission of Inquiry into the Actions of Canadian Officials in Relation to Maher Arar, Report of the Events Relating to Maher Arar: Factual Background, Volume I (Ottawa: Publishing and Depository Services, Public Works and Government Services Canada, 2006); Commission of Inquiry into the Actions of Canadian Officials in Relation to Maher Arar, Report of the Events Relating to Maher Arar: Factual Background, Volume II (Ottawa: Publishing and Depository Services, Public Works and Government Services Canada, 2006).

[12] I am indebted here to the insights of Peter Seixas. See Seixas's use of Nisga'a territorial claims in British Columbia as a spring-board to his exploration of the different ways that history may be taught

in secondary schools. Peter Seixas, "Schweigen! die Kinder! Or, Does Postmodern History Have a Place in the Schools?" in Peter N. Stearns, Peter Seixas, and Sam Wineburg, eds., Knowing, Teaching and Learning History: National and International Perspectives (New York: New York University Press, 2000).

[13] See Granatstein's comments on the questionable value of much of social history in Christopher Moore, "The Organized Man," The Beaver 71 (April-May 1991), 59.

[14] Following a reorganization of the NFB Web site, the Teachers' Centre was rendered inactive.

[15] According to Douglas Cremer, active learning, a multicultural emphasis and the use of computer technology, when taken together, may be considered "new foundational concepts" for teaching history. Douglas J. Cremer, "Matter, Method and Machine: The Synergy of World History, Active Learning, and Computer Technology," in Dennis A. Trinkle and Scott A. Merriman, eds., History.edu: Essays on Teaching with Technology (Armonk, NY: M.E. Sharpe, 2001), 120.

REFERENCES

Borden, R. L. (1938). *Robert Laird Borden: His memoirs*. Toronto, ON: The Macmillan Company.

Boulanger, C. (2004). *Readings in Quebec history*. Retrieved June 1, 2008, from http://www.marionopolis.edu./quebechistory/docs/October

Brown, R. C. (1980). *Robert Laird Borden: A biography, Volume 1*. Toronto, ON: The Macmillan Company.

Brunet, M. (1963). *Histoire du Canada par les texts* (Texte No. 93, pp. 238–240). Ottawa, ON: Fides.

Fowler, R. (1995). Teaching national consciousness in Canada: The role of mythology and history. *Canadian Social Studies, 29*(2), 63–65.

Gardner, H. (1998). Foreword. In D. Allen (Ed.), *Assessing student learning: From grading to understanding* (p. viii). New York: Teachers College Press.

Gee, J. P. (2003). *What video games have to teach us about learning and literacy*. New York: Palgrave Macmillan.

Gerus, O. W., & Rea, J. E. (1985). *The Ukrainians in Canada*. Ottawa, ON: Canadian Historical Association.

Granatstein, J. L. (1998). *Who killed Canadian history?* Toronto, ON: HarperCollins.

Granatstein, J. L., & Johnson, G. A. (1988). The evacuation of the Japanese Canadians, 1942: A realist critique of the received version. In N. Hillmer, et al. (Eds.), *On guard for thee: War, ethnicity, and the Canadian state, 1939–1945* (pp. 101–129). Ottawa, ON: Canadian Committee for the History of the Second World War.

Lee, P. (1998). Making sense of historical accounts. *Canadian Social Studies, 32*(2), 53–74.

Lee, P., & Ashby, R. (2000). Progression in historical understanding among students ages 7–14. In P. Stearns, P. Seixas, & S. Wineburg (Eds.), *Knowing, teaching and learning history: National and international perspectives* (pp. 210–231). New York: New York University Press.

Levin, M. A. (1969). Analysis of public issues: An interdisciplinary focus for Canadian studies. *Canadian Journal of History and Social Science, 5*(1), 75–92.

Levin, M. A., Newmann, F., & Oliver, D. W. (1969). *A three year law and social science curriculum for the high school* (Cooperative Research Report). Washington, DC: U.S. Office of Education.

Martynowych, O. T. (1991). *Ukrainians in Canada: The formative period, 1891–1924*. Edmonton, AB: Canadian Institute of Ukrainian Studies Press.

Melnycky, P. (1983). The internment of Ukrainians in Canada. In F. Swyripa & J. H. Thompson (Eds.), *Loyalties in conflict: Ukrainians in Canada during the Great War*. Edmonton, AB: Canadian Institute of Ukrainian Studies.

McKillop, A. B. (1999). Who killed Canadian history? A view from the trenches. *Canadian Historical Review, 80*(2), 269–299.

McLeod, R. C. (1982). History in Canadian secondary schools. *Canadian Historical Review, 63*(4).

Murrary, J. (1997). *Hamlet on the Holodeck: The future of narrative in cyberspace*. Cambridge, MA: MIT Press.

Oliver, D. W., & Shaver, J. P. (1966). *Teaching public issues in the high school*. Boston: Houghton Mifflin.

Peppin, P. (1993). Emergency legislation and rights in Canada: The War Measures Act and civil liberties. *Queen's Law Journal, 18*(1), 133–155.

Singleton, L. R. (2001). Following a tragic event: A necessary challenge for civic educators. *Social Education, 65*(7), 413–418.

Taylor, S. (1998). Globalization and the future of Canada. *Queen's Quarterly, 105*(3), 331–342.

Weinberger, D. (2002). *Small pieces loosely joined: A unified theory of the web*. Cambridge, MA: Perseus Publishing.

Yasnowskyj, P. (1978). Internment. In H. Piniuta (Ed.), *Land of pain, land of promise: First person accounts by Ukrainian pioneers, 1891–1914*. Saskatoon, SK: Western Producer Prairie Books.

Kevin Kee
Brock University
Canada

4. COMPUTERS AND THE MANAGEMENT OF LEARNING IN DISTANCE EDUCATION

How Students Construe Themselves in this Universe

WHAT IS A LEARNING MANAGEMENT SYSTEM?

Learning Management System (LMS) is a new term not yet widely used. Such systems are designed to solve several crucial tasks on various educational levels: administration, accounting, student management (progression, examination, grading), teaching, and facilitation of learning activities, as well as act as tools for the creation of content. LMSs are used in all education levels, as well as for training in larger businesses or industry. By 2002 more than 70% of all higher education institutions in the UK, Australia, and Canada had implemented an LMS, according to Coates, James, and Baldwin (2005).

Typically students who enrol in a course that use an LMS to any degree might be able to download slides, texts, or pictures that can support or fill the role of teaching. In other words, this is a "classroom" in which they can communicate live or asynchronously with teachers or classmates, or both simultaneously. They can also be assessed by way of tests, quizzes, portfolios, and written papers.

For training in large commercial organizations, Moran (2002) notes that LMS automate the administration, tracking, and reporting of classroom and online training events, enabling detailed analysis of the effectiveness of the training investment. Reasons given by many higher education institutions for implementing an LMS include: first, a promised reduction of instructional and testing costs; second, that multimedia can supply more comprehensible material adjusted to a wider range of learning styles; and third, students will have access to computers and software that are industry-standard as a preparation to work-life. As Coates et al. (2005) note:

> LMS's may appear to offer a means of regulating and packaging pedagogical activities by offering templates that assure order and neatness, and facilitate the control of quality. The perceived order created in teaching and learning by LMS is, we suspect, one of the more persuasive reasons for their rapid uptake. (p. 25)

The use of LMSs has become common in higher education and is also expanding significantly in primary and secondary schools where the technology provides tools for supervision, tutoring, and assessment. LMSs also supply tools for gathering and systematising data to be used for diagnostic testing of learning styles and preferences, testing of learning dysfunction and obstacles to learning, measurement of activities such as downloading frequencies, participation in interactions, and

T. Di Petta (Ed.), The Emperor's New Computer: ICT, Teachers and Teaching, 45–55.

compiling grades, and other wider sets of indicators of learning progress that might become available in unintended ways.

There is reason to be cautious about this increasingly widespread use of LMS. Several studies suggest that hackers and hostile guests easily intrude into LMS-systems as well as other computing systems vital to educational institutions. Security issues are gradually being taken more seriously (Branigan, 2004; Schneier, 2004). Further, Noble (2001) notes that those using the LMS system called *VirtualU* have required that students agree to the company's ownership of written communication on the LMS for the purpose of research and development. This surrendering of student copyright underlines the need for a critical review of the ethical and legal matters regarding the use of this kind of LMS.

So far, discussion in this area has focussed on student responsibilities for "netiquette" or "good behavior." As Barbara Sharf (1999) argues the field is in need of an ethics that goes beyond netiquette (see also Elgesem, 2001; Kitto, 2003; Selwyn, 2000; Vetlesen, 2003; Zembylas & Vrasidas, 2005). We also wondered if the students were hesitant to use LMS. It has been often reported that students use LMSs with less enthusiasm than what has been hoped for by the educational institution offering them (Haugsbakk, 2003). With these perspectives on LMS in mind we undertook to study an LMS system widely used in Norway called *ClassFronter*.

ClassFronter was developed in the late 1990s and since then has achieved commercial success. It has a substantial coverage of educational institutions in Scandinavia, in Europe, as well as in Asia. It is one of the competitors of *Blackboard*, *WebCT*, and *FirstClass* . It is the dominant provider to Norwegian educational institutions and was used by the college we approached for our study. We were interested in asking the students how they reasoned and acted ethically when using the LMS. What kinds of ideas did they operate with? What were their concerns and anxieties? What kind of problems did they see? Which did they accept, ignore, or refute? Did they see the LMS as helpful – or adding extra burdens?

LMS IN ACTION IN HIGHER EDUCATION: A STUDY OF THE *CLASSFRONTER* SYSTEM IN NORWAY

We interviewed 14 students enrolled in a three-year distance-based BA programme in nursing over a span of four years. Each group we interviewed gathered in its usual "seminar-room," sitting round a table with a minidisk-recorder and a microphone in the centre. The interviews took from 50-70 minutes. Students were almost mid-way into their distance education course on nursing. The course was arranged so that students could meet from time to time in a group room – access for group members, tutor, and ICT-manager; a regional room – access for all three groups, tutor, headmaster, and ICT-manager; and a plenary room – access for all students, tutors, teachers and ICT-manager.

The interviews were transferred to a computer as sound files and analysed using Qualitative Media Analyser (QMA) which allows the researcher to code the taped interview as sequences of sound. We used the interview guide as our coding instrument so that the topics dealt with in one interview could be detached and grouped with the same sections of the other interviews. QMA allowed us to compare similarly coded areas in the interviews rapidly. Relevant areas for quotations were transcribed.

Before admission to the study students were required to have a PC with Internet provision. All students used their PC at home, but none had any formal training nor described themselves as experienced in the use of ICT. A majority said they had no or almost no experience using ICT: 5 had never used a computer, 7 had used it, but only rarely, and 2 had used a computer at least twice a week before starting the course.

What then did the students tell us?

How Does It Feel to Be Visible?

We found that the students were aware that registered users were involved in the use of the program and that such users could have access to what transpired in the system. They believed that only registered names and authorities could inspect their activities. They said that they were suspicious if a new name popped up in the list of people with access (which might happen if a new tutor was assigned, and not properly introduced). While they think this learning environment is safe, they are aware of the uncertainties regarding the use of ICT: "I never trust computers" and "you never know" – are comments they made. They blame lack of formal knowledge and understanding of ICT and the Internet for not bringing to their attention more critical aspects of "risks," "security," and "caution" in this context. In everyday use they were more concerned with the elementary problems of making the computer work, "hitting the right buttons," getting "in and out," in other words with the minimal preconditions for using the computer. They know that the teacher and the tutor can survey their behavior inside the LMS but have not reflected on how this could affect them.

When they sense they are registered on the system or "seen," they do not think of this as being under surveillance. Being observed is interpreted in a positive sense: as "being helped," and "being responded to." Because of this positive interpretation they express a desire to "have more of it." Although they have computers at home, none subscribe to a view that the college "has moved into their home." They do not see this as an invasion of their private space. On the contrary, they think of it as a positive element, a timesaving and practical tool which they can handle in between other daily tasks.

The students do not think that their visible activity on the LMS will have any consequence for how teachers and tutors evaluate their development as students of nursing. They have only vaguely felt that their tutors have "pushed" them to become more engaged and interested in using the LMS as extensions of their subject-oriented engagement. The students do not see participation in the virtual room as particularly important for their learning. They see the core of their studying as reading, taking notes, doing assignments, and participating in the group activities.

Everything else is extra. Acting on the net for the purpose of being observed would be superficial and insignificant.

Making oneself visible through contributions via the LMS was, for most of the students, embarrassing: "I feel I open myself to the whole county," one student stated. Some students expressed strongly that they avoided writing for the discussion forum for the whole class because they disliked the idea of presenting themselves as ambitious or "better than others." They suggested that if they could use nicknames or just their initials, they might be more daring. The embarrassment of displaying oneself was generally seen as difficult to break away from. Several said they had ended their practice of writing occasionally for the forum, and would rather send private e-mails to the tutor. To write for the large forum, they needed to polish their message in advance, preparing it first with paper and pencil. But still they expressed admiration for the students who wrote freely for the forum. They expressed a wish for more contributions and more contributors, which would lower their own thresholds for writing "in the open."

Students interpret the function of teachers observing them, registering their participation and presence (visible and invisible) in the virtual rooms, as positive. They are content with the idea of being seen as intimately joined with feeling secure, being assured and checked for the quality of their statements, and being looked after. They feel inhibited in the matter of being constructive and willing participants because the visibility of being on the net is an embarrassment. They have a strong fear of being unveiled: "I would rather send my question on the e-mail – everybody knows this except me." They do not see becoming visible as a strategy to please the teachers. They do not find the presence of the computer in their home as a threat or improper invasion of privacy. "It is more embarrassing to pass the book-shelf with all our [unread] textbooks on it" – one student said. "Being a student implies there are always numerous challenges to do things, it isn't bothering that a teacher observes you."

How Should One Behave on the Net? The Question of "Nettiquette"

These students unanimously agreed that messages containing personal or private information should not be sent. They considered the LMS as a "formal area" – a school – where only strictly subject-related topics should be dealt with. If personal or private information was relevant, it should be discussed in an e-mail or in private with tutors or fellow students. Conflicts and problems within the group should not be dealt with inside the LMS because it would be uncomfortable to have to deal with such unpleasant topics in writing. They also felt that writing in itself would cause more misunderstandings than contribute to the solving of problems.

Even if there were better learning activities or more invitations to participate in various discussion groups, these students would probably decline to participate. Their lack of time restrained their activities in many ways. During the practicum, they said they would rarely open the LMS. On one occasion, when a teacher gave them an "Easter-quiz" unexpectedly, they were irritated when the teachers later on asked why so few had completed the test. They felt this behavior was improper and unsuitable. But they also felt the challenge, and would eventually take the test, but not until they felt safe enough. Even if they thought this test had no significance for their formal evaluation, most of them abstained feeling that the instructor had no justification for requiring the quiz.

At the same time they were genuinely sceptical of their own participation in the LMS. They consider it as a risk-taking activity. Several of them claimed they would rather work thoroughly with even the simplest texts, rewriting outlines until they found it worthy of submission: "I regret a posting whenever I see my name attached to it." They refrain from entering personal or private information: "One simply doesn't write about one's Granddad on the net." As a group they reported that they were so cautious that they had little reason to regret or want anything undone, yet, some said they had regrets because they had been too incautious.

All the students point out the lack of time as the main reason for their constant sense of being inadequate in front of the computer. They supposed more up-to-date computers and equipment would make it easier (faster) to spend more time on the net. They also felt they had to give priority to other tasks and demands in their family life or at work. They just felt they did not have the time.

As a whole, the students reveal a wide range of ethical issues that concern them. They gladly accept the formal restrictions – the surveillance and management – for the benefits they get. They put great trust in the institutional framework, and in the expertise of their teachers. They make a distinct separation between their identity as students and as private individuals. They are uneasy if teachers or fellow students cross lines that demarcate areas of formal and informal information. They are careful about misleading other students by presenting information that could be wrong or inadequate.

It appears that the students were concerned with the fact that what they wrote as contributors to discussion groups would be significant for the other readers. They wrote their messages with care, anxious that their information might be ambiguous or misleading, or be a source for misunderstandings: "It is so easy to misunderstand what is written," one stated. They eagerly wanted the teachers to read and participate in order to have their material checked and inspected for the quality: "I am petrified by the thought that what I wrote might be completely wrong." Participating teachers relieved this anxiety. On the other hand, if the teachers initiated responses, they admitted that replying in a sense was replying to the teachers, forgetting that "all the others" could – and would be - reading it. They tried to write in ways that did not reveal doubts or second thoughts, unless it was for the group's own discussion "room." The formal level of the forum matters greatly, and one group – where the members lived some distance from each other had developed a chat-like style of communication. The students said they had tried the chat-function, but were not particularly pleased with how it worked. Writing is a serious business, they said: "I could never have written about conflicts – having it there on the screen would mean it was very serious and public – for every body – you never know…"

The students express a very serious and strict attitude towards how to communicate in the virtual room. They unanimously express that messages containing personal or private information should not come to the fore. They refrain from entering personal or private information. They report than they are so cautious that they have little reason to regret or want anything undone.

WHAT ISSUES DO THESE STUDENTS PRESENT US WITH?

This case study shows us that these part-time students think about ethical matters in many facets. We were surprised that these matters were of such strong concern. We found that their suspicion is well founded. We have categorized what the students told us into three areas of concern about LMS. These are being observed, coping with a fractured work style, and being judged.

Being and Being Observed

We read the students' concern also as a rejection of some basic presuppositions inherent in the LMS; for instance, a concern about being observed. As has been noted by Burbules and Callister Jr. (2000), few are so closely monitored as students in ordinary schooling; behavior, attitudes, and performance are constantly watched and graded. In that respect, the introduction of an LMS does not represent a novelty but an augmentation of the potential exercising powers of technology. An awareness of this augmentation can be seen in what these students say. They see how surveillance can have a positive influence on their forming of a community of students, which empowers them in fulfilling a complex everyday life. On the other hand, students seek refuge from this surveillance, physically as well as emotionally. The success of many teaching approaches using LMS depends on open and unconditional communication about subject issues, which caters for dialogical processes by which students construct meaning socially, and from diverse social and cultural backgrounds.

In some fundamental respects this presupposes the "Ideal Speech Situation" based on rational communicative actions, in a Habermasian context (Heslep, 2001), which should eliminate strategic communication. Sincere, immediate openness, which promotes social presence, often self-disclosing examples, and personal experiences, are features of the "on-line" pedagogy, highly valued by both students and tutors. This presupposition contrasts with centuries of educational experience in which the relationship between students and teachers has been deemed to involve deep conflict (Ong, 1974). The students we interviewed kept a respectful distance from their teachers. Teachers assigning fun but nevertheless challenging and unexpected tasks to the students are resisted. Using the LMS for unsolicited or less serious comments is not accepted easily.

So, in spite of almost a generation of theories dictating social openness and easy going chatting as fundamental to the social climate of discussion groups (Rovai, 2002), these students claim there are ethical concerns that keep them back from engaging in a more open and self-disclosing climate of communication. They stick to seriousness and down-to-earth realism. These students do not play with their identity as Turkle (1995) suggested Internet users might do, at least not more than is strictly needed. The strategic ways students use to present themselves are decided by the anticipated reactions of the "others" that constitute the social group. According to Turkle, these self-presentations are playful and testing, yet the students we talked to show more caution because there are always ways to detect the identity of the student in an LMS. Strategic behavior will tempt students to appear more active than they would otherwise be (visiting more discussion groups, downloading more documents), but certain activities would be more likely to be observed and regulated by the social group: what, when, and how to contribute to discussion groups, for instance. They will be exposed to crossing expectations: to be active and self-assured towards the teacher/tutor and self-restricted and modest towards fellow students.

Coping with a Disjoined Working Group

Knowing the social norms about what to say and how to behave were crucial to these students. Establishing trust with fellow students and teachers was important, but intimate or self-disclosing communication was to be restricted to e-mails. These students demonstrated a high degree of awareness of how the teachers monitor and control the student progress, test scores, completion, attendance, and participation in social learning contexts. Their rejection of becoming more involved than necessary is, we think, a way of resisting the hegemony of the teacher. But students also accept that the liberty they have gained by being able to stay home with their family and keep up their ordinary lives has a price. Teaching and learning are no longer subordinated to the limits and structures of the life on campus. Teaching is offered in flexible ways in regard to how, when, or where studies are accomplished. The liberation from fixed places, routines, and times gives a greater degree of freedom from the ritual control and limitations conventionally exercised at the campus. "Flexibility" is the "buzzword." What about flexibility?

Sennet (1998) suggests that the "new organization" of people's workplaces in electronic commuting, office-less bureaucracies, results in an organization which is totally invisible, yet highly connected and with an efficient infra-structure. When we try to trace the "discontinual reorganization" of work in "late modernity," we surely see parallels to how these students organise their lives. The single students are placed in observable cells which are inspected regularly by the tutors/teachers, physically outside the college, but in the "virtual" realm of a truly "invisible college," tied to the college by the "strength of weak ties." What Sennet claims about the reshaping of working life we see paralleled in education. Adult students must adapt to a triple identity as parent, worker, – and student. While campus students participate in a rich social environment related to study, being a distance student implies being void of the contexts students normally use for negotiation between the existential demands of the subject in question and her/his self.

Searching for an interpretative community of fellow students is easier if the students are organised in projects or collaborative groups and/or have access to communicative areas such as a homepage or an LMS. Instead of being physically in the college, visiting classes, discussing in lunch breaks and formal meetings, manoeuvring in a set of visible and distinct rules and expectancies, the distance student in general confronts either blurred and invisible rules, or overly rigid and visible regulations. While flexibility of "virtual learning spaces" appears as a generous offer of adjustment and pragmatism, it also enrols adult students in new structures of management and control.

LMS is more than a "mind tool"; it also controls numerous new tasks of monitoring and surveying the flow of examinations, tests, and portfolios, which reflects the needs of the modern university as "knowledge business." LMS allows tutors to influence styles of communication and link persons according to similar measures, as well as terminate relations that are rendered undesirable. The tutor's technical potential for analysing processes apart from results produces overview and knowledge about a wider repertoire of the person's character and abilities related to productivity and process-capabilities, and enhances the options for more productive re-engineering of groups and sequences of production. Again this can make the learning process more productive, and saves money and energy. Testing, measuring, and evaluating are essential dimensions for the making of the single student as a controllable unit of a cell in which the student knows he/she is observed.

Our interpretation is that these students see themselves as negotiating practical adaptations to this flexible reorganization. They count gains and losses, use the good opportunities and avoid the excesses.

Being Classified

When students fail to engage in discussion groups this has been interpreted as a problem with either the technology, or with the social set-up of the distance education programme. But these students have grave concerns about how such discussions might produce misunderstandings, illegitimate norms, misbehavior, and improper language. One source of concern is the process of moderation itself. As Selwyn (2000) notes, in his analysis of the British "National Grid for Learning" (a portal for teachers, students, and school administrators in the UK), the editorial function in discussion and special interest groups is quite remarkably unofficial and unfocused. By selecting and omitting perspectives, points of view, and descriptions of particular practices, the editor sets distinct norms for behavior, attitudes, and recommended practices within the limited frames set by the editor.

The student's identity in these groups is not achieved by virtue of social status, gender, tradition, or geography, but by ways of self-presentation or posing: by making oneself seen or observable. The educational system is an important arena for learning to do this. Each student is exposed to evaluation and examination, followed by classification and differentiation, leading to a codified documented individuality (Marshall, 1996). When teaching and learning is withdrawn from the possibilities of control dictated by the conventional context of the campus with its social presence and space/time routines, electronically based control moves in. This control is experienced by the student as a need for being included in some way or other, to be controlled and observed, to receive feed-back and get a sense of belonging, of progression and social relations to fellow students. The teachers' or tutors' gaze becomes important for motivation and confirmation of their status as students. This is a game these students resent. They would rather abstain from being classified in invisible ways.

What Kind of a World does LMS Create?

The comprehensive analysis of e-learning by Zemsky and Massy (2004) concluded that e-learning has ended as a thwarted innovation. They say that e-learning has become a conservative force making it easier to deliver material and manage classes more effectively but not support difficult activities such as building trust and allowing the expression of ideas without fear (See also Rønning & Grepperud, 2006).

Mark Poster (1990, 1996) has described the surveillance function of ICT as a "SuperPanopticon" in which traces and activities of a person on the Internet can be retrieved and combined by using computers. In the form of a Learning Management System we have the perfect tool for such purposes (Land & Baine, n.d.). Nevertheless, even if students do understand the risks in using an LMS, Tu (2002) suggests that students may too easily involve themselves in "risk-taking activities" on the net (See also Knutson, 2002).

However, the students we interviewed expressed caution and said they avoided risks. Cheeky or impolite utterances were effectively censored due to norms held by the students themselves. There might be cultural differences here. Research suggests there are differences in communicative styles, both between ethnical and national cultures (Carr-Chellman, 2005; Gunawardena et al., 2001). These Norwegian students bring their cultural assumptions and behavior with them to the LMS, and this culture does not seem to support easy going talk, chats, speculations, and exploratory or imaginative descriptions. This might also be a help in protecting them from the SuperPanopticon.

The careful ethical consideration students evinced during the interviews reveal that fundamental ethical questions are important to them. Their ideas were reflections on their experience as members of a social group existing on the web, establishing a new set of social relations which demand explicit norms, values, and ethical considerations. Their experience leads us to suggest that discussions concerning surveillance and Learning Management Systems need to be encouraged. Some ethical directions are found in the ethical guidelines for research (Elgesem, 2001; Sharf, 1999). The students we interviewed expressed their ethical standards about their behavior on the net, and they also evinced an awareness of the risks connected with using the Internet.

They did not conceive of their registration on or management through the LMS as surveillance, but rather as an expression of institutional care. It is a fair conclusion to draw from this that their general strategy of minimising their exposure to the visible areas of the LMS, and the fact that the teachers were not challenging this behavior and avoided making more activity on the discussion groups obligatory or compulsory, make these risks less salient than they might be. Certainly this dichotomy will need further examination and research.

REFERENCES

Branigan, C. (2004). CoSN issues cyber security resources. *eSchool News online*. Retrieved October 9, 2006, from http://www.eschoolnews.com/news/showStoryts.cfm?ArticleID=5271

Burbules, N. C., & Callister, T. A., Jr. (2000). *Watch IT: The risks and promises of information technologies for education*. Boulder, CO: Westview Press.

Carr-Chellman, A. (2005). *Global perspectives on e-learning rhetoric and reality*. Thousand Oaks, CA: Sage.

Coates, H., James, R., & Baldwin, G. (2005). A critical examination of the effects of learning management systems on university teaching and learning. *Tertiary Education and Management, 11*(1), 19–36.

Elgesem, D. (2001). *What is special about the ethical issues in online research?* Retrieved February 19, 2003, from http://www.nyu.edu/projects/nissenbaum/ethics_elg_full.html

Gunawardena, C. N., Nolla, A. C., Wilson, P. L., Lopez-Islas, J. R., Ramirez-Angel, N., & Megchun-Alzipar, R. M. (2001). A cross-cultural study of group process and development in online conferences. *Distance Education, 22*(1), 85–121.

Haugsbakk, G. (2003). Problemer i paradis? Eller: Hvorfor gjør ikke studentene som vi sier de skal gjøre? [Problems in paradise, Or: Why don't students do what they are told?]. In Y. Fritze, G. Haugsbakk, & Y. T. Nordkvelle (Eds.), *Dialog og nærhet, IKT og undervisning [Dialogue and presence, ICT and teaching]* (pp. 109–124). Kristiansand, Norway: HøyskoleForlaget.

Heslep, R. D. (2001). Habermas on communication in teaching. *Educational Theory, 51*(2), 191–207.

Kitto, S. (2003). Translating an electronic panopticon: Educational technology and the re-articulation of lecturer-student relations in online learning. *Information, Communication & Society, 6*(1), 1–23.

Knutson, D. S. (2002). "The young are rude today": Reflections on distance-delivered courses. *Kairos, 6*(2). Retrieved March 1, 2006, from http://english.ttu.edu/kairos/6.2/binder2.html?coverweb/de/knutson/index.htm

Land, R., & Bayne, S. (n.d.). *Screen or monitor? Surveillance and disciplinary power in online learning environments*. Retrieved October 4, 2006, from http://www.malts.ed.ac.uk/staff/sian/surveillancepaper.htm

Marshall, J. D. (1996). *Michel Foucault: Personal autonomy and education*. Dordrecht, The Netherlands: Kluwer Academic.

Moran, J. V. (2002). *Mission: Buy an LMS*. Retrieved October 8, 2006, from http://www.learningcircuits.org/2002/jan2002/moran.html

Noble, D. (2001). *Digital diploma mills: The automation of higher education*. New York: Monthly Press.

Ong, W. (1974). Agonistic structures in academia: Past to present. *Dædalus, 104*(4), 229–238.

Poster, M. (1990). *The mode of information: Poststructuralism and social context*. Cambridge: Polity Press.

Poster, M. (1996). Databases as discourse; or, electronic interpellations. In D. Lyon & E. Zureik (Eds.), *Computers, surveillance, and privacy* (pp. 175–192). Minneapolis, MN: University of Minnesota Press.

Rovai, A. P. (2002). Building sense of community at a distance. *International Review of Research In Open and Distance Learning, 3*(1), 1–16.

Rønning, W. M., & Grepperud, G. (2006). The everyday use of ICT in Norwegian flexible education. *Seminar.net*, (1). 2 Retrieved October 8, 2006, from http://www.seminar.net/current-issue/the-everyday-use-of-ict-in-norwegian-flexible-education

Schneier, B. (2004). *Secrets and lies: Digital security in a networked world*. Indianapolis, IL: Wiley.

Selwyn, N. (2000). Creating a "connected" community? Teachers' use of an electronic discussion group. *Teachers College Record, 102*(4), 750–778.

Sharf, B. (1999). Beyond netiquette: The ethics of doing naturalistic discourse research on the internet. In S. Jones (Ed.), *Doing internet research* (pp. 243–256). London: Sage.

Sennet, R. (1998). *The corrosion of character: The personal consequences of work in the new capitalism*. New York: W.W. Norton.

Tu, C.-H. (2002). The relationship between social presence and online privacy. *The Internet and Higher Education, 5*(4), 293–318.

Turkle, S. (1995). *Life on the screen: Identity in the age of the internet.* New York: Simon and Schuster.

Vetlesen, A. J. (2003). Det forpliktende møte [The committing encounter]. In Y. Fritze, G. Haugsbakk, & Y. T. Nordkvelle (Eds.), *Dialog og nærhet, IKT og undervisning* [Dialogue and presence, ICT and teaching]. Kristiansand, Norway: HøyskoleForlaget.

Zembylas, M., & Vrasidas, C. (2005). Levinas and the "inter-face": The ethical challenge of online education. *Educational Theory, 55*(1), 61–78.

Zemsky, R., & Massy, W. F. (2004). *Thwarted innovation. What happened to e-learning and why?* Retrieved March 1, 2006, from http://www.irhe.upenn.edu/Docs/Jun2004/ThwartedInnovation.pdf

Yngve Troye Nordkvelle
Lillehammer University College
Norway

Randi Tosterud
Gjøvik University College
Norway

5. AN AFRICAN CONTRIBUTION TOWARDS AN EMERGENT PHILOSOPHY OF MOBILE LEARNING

INTRODUCTION

Mobile learning, or m-learning, is learning that is accomplished with the use of small, data-centric handheld computer-communicators. These portable digital communicating devices, which Diana Oblinger (2007, p. 16) colloquially refers to as "personal life remote controls," usually include smartphones, personal digital assistants (PDAs), other portable handheld devices[1], and wireless two-way internet connections. M-learning has seen exponential growth in recent years, and increasing availability of high bandwidth network infrastructures, advances in wireless technologies and popularity of handheld devices have opened up new accessibility opportunities for education.

Despite recent attempts to put an assortment of aspects with regard to m-learning in a variety of theoretical and philosophical perspectives, there is a dearth of literature as far as studying m-learning from a hermeneutically reconstructive, social epistemological perspective is concerned. The work of Anderson and Elloumi (2004), Barker, Krull, and Mallinson (2005), Clough (2005), Curtis, Luchini, bobrowsky, Quintana, and Soloway (2002), Danesh, et al. (2001), Engeström (2003), Keegan (2003), Laouris and Eteokleous (2005), Nichols (2003), Nyíri (2002), Prensky (2001), Scanlon, Jones, and Waycott (2005), Sharples (2000, 2003, 2005a, 2005b), Sharples, Taylor, and Vavoula (2005), Taylor, Sharples, O'Malley, Vavolua, and Waycott (2006), Waycott (2004), and Zurita and Nussbaum (2004) – to name but a few – is ample proof of this.

The following question, in particular, has thus far remained unanswered:

How may an African understanding of basic philosophic-anthropological categories, such as: (a) being human (humanness) as becoming human (humanisation), (b) learners as openness to being, (c) learners as searching for and finding meaning, (d) learners as social beings, and (e) learners' existence as an existence "caught in values" contribute to the development of a future philosophy of m-learning?

Most of the available literature on m-learning is still very much practice-based and is typically presented in a descriptive format. This is patent from the work of, for example, Becta (2004), Belt (2001), Beute (2004), Chang, Sheu, and Chan (2003), Juniu (2003), K12 Handhelds (2004), Liu, et al. (2003), Perry (2003), Roschelle (2003), Stead (2004), Thornton and Houser (2004), Vahey and Crawford (2003), and

T. Di Petta (Ed.), The Emperor's New Computer: ICT, Teachers and Teaching, 57–75.

Wood (2003). The result is that a conspicuous lack of an established philosophy of m-learning continues to exist (Anderson & Elloumi, 2004, p. 33; Nichols, 2003, p. 1). This has led to current practices where the use of mobile technology in educational settings tends – increasingly – to be technology-led rather than philosophy-led or theory-led (Nichols, 2003, p. 1; Ravenscroft, 2001, pp. 133–156; Watson, 2001, p. 251). One of the latest examples is the *Handheld Augmented Reality Project* (HARP), which is a collaboration among Harvard University, the Massachusetts Institute of Technology (MIT), and the University of Wisconsin at Madison. It uses wireless handheld computers to enhance teaching and learning through a series of activities that draw on the attributes of individual learners' surroundings (Devaney, 2007).

This paper suggests an African contribution towards an emergent philosophy of m-learning that may eventually be employed as an educational positioning system for policy-makers, curriculum-designers, educational quality assurors, and other m-learning stakeholders and role-players.

OUTLINE AND ORGANIZATION OF PAPER

After contextualising this study, I follow up my comments on the methodology which I have employed with a discussion of the following interrelated introductory aspects of an African contribution towards an emergent philosophy of m-learning: (a) the differences between a Western and an African life and worldview, (b) the differences between a Western and an African view of humanness and humanity, (c) the differences between a Western and an African ontology, (d) the differences between a Western and an African view of learning, (e) the differences between a Western and an African view of ambient learning, and (f) some concluding remarks about the significance of an African life and worldview for a future philosophy of m-learning. Figure 1 below shows the sequential arrangement of these six aspects. It also demonstrates how they hermeneutically relate to each other for the purpose of this paper:

I will end the discussion of each of the first five aspects with a few critical questions that emanate from the preceding discussion. I then round off this paper with a few concluding remarks.

CONTEXTUALISING THIS STUDY

Since the advent of data-centric handheld computer-communicators (such as mobile phones) that are technologically capable of capturing and transmitting audio files and/or video clips, the world has been witnessing the emergence of teenage civilian journalism – a panoptic phenomenon that sees learners of school-going age straying into the province of trained journalists. Mobile phones equipped with audio-recording capability and cameras have brought the Napoleonic gaze into

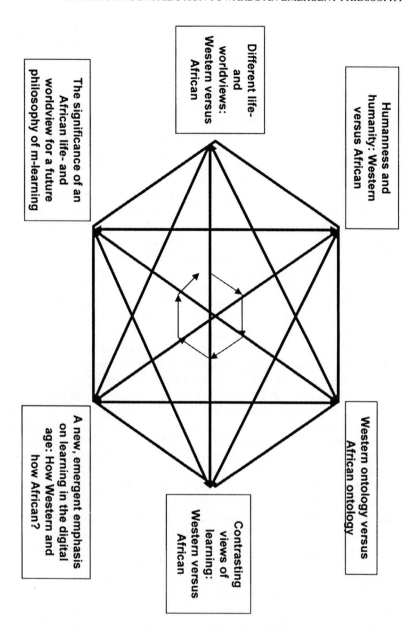

Figure 1. A few introductory aspects of an African contribution towards an emergent philosophy of m-learning: sequence and interrelatedness.

every teenager's pocket, allowing children of the digital age to become civilian journalists or even directors, producers, and stars of their own dramas by simply pressing a button (Tsimitakis, 2006).

On January 31, 2007, it was, for example, reported that Milwaukee (USA) will have banned the use of mobile phones from 217 of its schools by Monday February 5, 2007, because: "cell phones created distractions or were used to cheat, take inappropriate photos or summon unwanted outsiders." Several American states, including Washington, Oregon, and Rhode Island are also considering bills that would curb or outlaw "cyber bullying," in which students taunt or insult their peers on social-networking web sites or through instant text messaging. Legislators and educators in America point to the growing need for guidelines outlining how to punish cyber and mobile bullying. They claim that this kind of behavior has gone unchecked for years, with few laws or policies on the books explaining how to treat it (eSchoolNews Online, 2007). The same is true in South Africa. Mestry, Van der Merwe, and Squelch (2006) demonstrate, for example, how incidences of teenage cyber bullying, instant text message-harassment, mobile phone-stalking, etc. are steadily on the increase in this country.

Despite the virtuous intentions of stakeholders and role-players in education, the manner in which some learners of school-going age are using mobile technology today is often far removed from what may be deemed educationally tenable, socially responsible, and morally commendable behavior. In spite of (and some may even argue *because of*) the nature and extent of the surveillance society we are living in, our learners are increasingly growing up in an epoch where humanistic values are decrementing and where a clear vision towards social progress seems to be gradually disintegrating (Laouris & Eteokleous, 2005, p. 10). Contemporary society is in dire need of "more peacemakers, healers, restorers, storytellers... of every shape and form... It needs people of moral courage willing to join the fight to make the world habitable and humane" (Orr, 1991, p. 55). Bandura (2002) even argues that "civilised life requires, in addition to humane personal codes, social systems that can uphold compassionate behaviour and renounce cruelty" (p. 116).

We are only just beginning to recognise and understand the impact that mobile technology – and especially mobile phone technology – is having on the education landscape. Our efforts to promote responsible m-learning praxis (where "praxis" is understood to comprise a cycle of action-reflection-action which is central to liberatory education) should, therefore, take into account the role that m-learning may be playing within any future framework of socially responsible education (Laouris, 2003). In order to accomplish this, teachers and educationists will need to reconceptualise, re-organise and re-narrate issues of "education," "teaching," "learning," "mobility," and "mobile technology" from a philosophically plausible point of departure. If m-learning is to mould an educationally justifiable niche in the pedagogical endeavours of developing countries such as South Africa, its philosophical underpinnings should be made explicit and available for critique (Berger, 2000; Nichols, 2003).

ON A METHODOLOGICAL NOTE

I describe and explore m-learning in this paper from a hermeneutically reconstructive and social epistemological perspective, outlining a few contours within which the development of a philosophy of m-learning may be contemplated. The rationale behind this is, firstly, my belief that m-learning is as much a social enterprise as it is an individual one. Secondly, I assume (based on my understanding of the available literature) that m-learning also socializes learners into the practices, values, tools, languages, and problems of the digital community. Thirdly, I believe that these assembled practices, values, tools, languages and problems with regard to m-learning "are themselves culturally and historically situated, carrying the wisdom and hidden life and worldview assumptions that went into their design. Thus they form a learning system with the learner, reorganizing action and determining what can be carried out" (Boote & Beile, 2006, p. 34).

Flowing from these first three explanations, my final (and overarching) reason is the fact that the available literature on m-learning is shaped mainly by Western researchers' histories and experiences, interacting with national and transnational imperatives and the now dominant neo-liberalist discourse. It openly favors a Western, technicist and individualist approach to m-learning and it is increasingly determining the conceptualisation of m-learning as discursive construct and its concomitant enactment in educational settings from a predominantly Western point of view. One of the most recent examples included the call for papers (by the Editorial Board) for a special issue of the *International Journal of Mobile Learning and Organisation* that was published early in 2008. This special issue of the IJMLO is entitled "Information and Service *Personalization* for Mobile Learning" [italics added].

Adopting a post-modern and – to some extent a – post-structuralist stance, I try to counteract this by regarding m-learning discourses in this paper as discursive constructions where meanings are emergent, deferred, and dispersed. I maintain that m-learning as discursive construct does not have independent, established, or prearranged status outside of the narratives and texts that constitute it (Westwood & Linstead, 2001). If m-learning is, for example, to be located epistemologically within the new, emergent emphasis of "ambient learning," it needs – in the interests of a more just and equitable society – to engage not only with competing life and worldview discourses, but also with competing discourses about humanness, humanity, and human learning and what they all may privilege.

I also maintain that our understanding of being human in terms of the real essentials of our human life-world should fundamentally influence our conceptualisation of m-learning. Consequently, I attempt to re-organise and re-narrate some of the fundamental aspects of an African life and worldview with a view to identifying their significance for a future philosophy of m-learning. From a structure-agency perspective (Bowles & Gintis, 1976), I also seek, meta-theoretically, to challenge the predominant neo-liberalist free-market discourse around and fundamental assumptions underpinning the idea of the so-called "autonomous, rational, possessive individual" (hereafter "ARPI"). Central to my argument is the hermeneutical challenge of trying to understand the African view of individual lives as being structurally determined, by asking how an African understanding of basic anthropological categories, such as: (a) being human (humanness) as becoming human (humanisation), (b) learners as openness to being, (c) learners as searching for and finding meaning, (d) learners as social beings, and (e) learners' existence as an existence "caught in values" may contribute to a future philosophy of m-learning.

I argue that a hermeneutically reconstructive and social epistemological perspective on m-learning should take account of the dialogic-diagogic nature of humanisation. Becoming human essentially involves a process of appealing and responding, of leading and guiding, of accompanying each other and of demonstrating solidarity, of cooperating in implicit trust, and of building and maintaining fiduciary alliances. By accepting that m-learning is a *means* of education as opposed to a *mode* of education (Nichols, 2003, p. 3), I propose that this may lead us to reconceptualise not only the future design and implementation of mobile technology but also of future m-learning praxis.

Finally, in this paper, I use the term m-learning only with reference to the pedagogical domain. I do not address the possible significance of m-learning for the andragogical or gerontagogical domains.

THE CHALLENGE: FROM A "WESTERN" PERSPECTIVE?

South Africa is still lacking a developed infrastructure for information and communication technologies (including mobile communication technologies) that is comparable with the best examples that are presently in use in industrialised, developed countries. This progressively widens the notorious "digital gap" between ourselves and the developed world.

In response to this under-development, South Africa has taken the initiative towards the adoption of a renewal framework, the *New Partnership for Africa's Development* (NEPAD), which identifies information and communication technologies (and, therefore, mobile learning technologies as well) as central in the struggle to reduce poverty on the continent. It is hoped that these technologies will boost optimism for overcoming barriers of social and geographical isolation, that they will increase access to information and education, and that they will enable the poor to participate in the making of decisions that have an impact on their lives (Draft White Paper on e-Education, 2003).

The reality, though, is that South Africa forms part of Africa and that the majority of Africans share a life and worldview that differs profoundly from the notion of the "ARPI" of the developed West[2]. Thinking about m-learning would, therefore, have to challenge the privileging power of indicators such as the Western, technicist and individualist approach to mobile technology and the use thereof. It will also have to challenge the privileging influence of the grand-narrative of neo-liberalist, free-market-ism on the shaping of m-learning discourses worldwide. I regard this as an ominous discursive pattern that is progressively heralding the dawn of technological neo-colonialism (in Africa). It ingeniously valorises good teaching and learning in terms of the availability – and subsequent use of – Westernized technological hardware such as data-centric handheld computer-communicators and it effectively marginalises the role that an African ontology (including an African ontology of learning) and an African view of humanity could play in this regard.

THE REALITY: DIFFERENT LIFE AND WORLDVIEWS

The acknowledgement of ethno-cultural differences between – in our case – fellow South Africans has been (and still is) equated with *racism*. These differences have, consequently, either been romanticised[3], or anxiously swept under the carpet (Van Niekerk, 1996, p. 2). The result was that neither their explosive value, nor their potential has received serious scholarly attention recently. The stark reality, though, is that the structure-agency debate and the growing tension between the life and worldviews of Africa and those of the "ARPI"s' of the West have far-reaching effects. The challenge is to discover patterns for cooperation and co-existence – especially as far as the ubiquitous use of interactive, data-centric, handheld computer-communicators (such as smartphones, personal digital assistants (PDAs), and similar portable handheld devices) in educational settings is concerned. One step towards accomplishing this task includes extending the structure-agency debate by contrasting a "Western" life and worldview with an "African" life and worldview.

In the "West," the two dominant mental trends of the past few centuries were (a) their faith in progress, competitiveness, and performativity and (b) their belief that they can gain control over the natural laws of the cosmos and that they can utilise it to build a better world. In this regard, the existence and use of interactive, data-centric, handheld computer-communicators may arguably serve as one of the best contemporary examples of these mental trends.

For "Africa," the dominant mental trend over the past centuries has been "the interconnectedness of all things" (Mphahlele, 1972; Wiredu, 1980, p. 4). Because of the interconnectedness of all things, it is impossible within the African cultural reality and experience to speak of, for example, mobile telephone technology as if it were detached from religion; of religion as if it were detached from mythology and speculative thought; of speculative thought as if it were detached from mythical feelings; and of these feelings as if they were detached from educational principles and political ideas (Broodryk, 2002, pp. 50–62, 2004, pp. 119–131; Mbigi, 2005, pp.

111–137; Mosley, 1995, pp. 301–310; Nkurunziza, 1989, pp. 129–170; Rush & Anyanwu, 1984, p. 81).

For the West, the dominant mental image is the arrow that speaks of eternal, purposeful progress, competitiveness, and perfomativity; a kind of Latinate *per aspera ad astra*. Our "Western" concept of time is, furthermore, also linear: a straight line – like a straight-flying arrow – from the past, through the present and onwards to the future. For Africa, though, it is rather like a Riceourian circle of fused existential time (Ochs, 1997, p. 191): past, present, and future are eternally interconnected and experienced as a kind of temporal simultaneity.

For "Africa," the dominant mental image is the circle that speaks of the yearning to find a home in one, big cosmic order; to reconcile all differences within this circle – not to control it (Van Niekerk, 1996, p. 115). The circle implies that contradictions are both sustained and accepted; that which was, will be again. There should be harmony and unity, instead of control, progress, competitiveness, and performativity for the sake of progress. For Africa, progress is never a linear process. Instead, as the Ghanese writer Kofi Awoonor (1976) points out, in Africa "the widening of the circle … ultimately … constitutes the only human progress" (p. 167).

From the discussion in this paragraph, the following two critical questions emerge:

– How may m-learning contribute to and promote the interconnectedness of all things?
– How may m-learning help to balance the human pursuit of eternal, purposeful progress, competitiveness, and performativity, on the one hand, with the human yearning to pursue harmony, unity, belonging and reconciliation on the other?

These profound differences between the life and worldview of the "ARPI" of the "West" and an "African" life and worldview also impact on Western and African views of humanness and humanity.

HUMANNESS AND HUMANITY: DESCARTES VERSUS AFRICA

Together with Descartes, "Westerners" still proclaim in a typically modernistic fashion: I *think*, therefore I am. In contrast, African philosophy originates from a collective mind and for the African, "I" pre-supposes a "We"; in fact I is contingent upon We. Africans therefore proclaim: (a) We belong, therefore we are – and as a consequence of which – I am, (b) I am because we are and since we are therefore I am, and even (c) "We feel, therefore I am" (Mazrui, 1978, p. 86). Africans are social beings that are in constant communion with one another. For them, a human being is only a human being through his or her relationships with other human beings (Eze, 2006, p. 4). It is interesting to note that this quintessentially African view of humanness and humanity resonates strongly with Jean-Paul Sartre's (1962) ontological category of *Für-Andere-Sein* (p. 299), namely that the fellow human being is co-constitutor of *my* being. What I am for my fellow human beings (Für-Andere-Sein) thus determines my being what I am and this implies that the "Being for Others" is indeed constitutive for what Sartre refers to as *Cogito préréflexif* or *Conscience (de) soi* (German: *Für-sich-Sein*).

The nature of a person's "being-in-the-world" is, therefore, such that by virtue of being a person, (s)he has embodied in his/her humanity other persons or beings that form part of his/her humanity: (s)he embodies in his/her person the whole of humanity in their differences and uniqueness (Eze, 2006, p. 83). This fundamental view of humanness and humanity is best articulated by the saying: *Umuntu ungumuntu ngabanye abantu* or *Motho ke motho ka batho ba bangwe.* These are, respectively, the IsiZulu and Sepedi versions of a traditional African aphorism, often translated as: "a person is a person through other persons" (Ramose, 1999, p. 49; Shutte, 1993, p. 46).

For "Africa," the main purpose is not to relentlessly progress, nor is it to (relentlessly) compete, or to (relentlessly) perform. For Africans, the main purpose is to belong: "this lead[s] him on to a sense of belonging in some ground pattern or design, a sense of continuity which connected him to his ancestors" (Mphahlele, 1972, p. 24). An African individual's humanness and humanity is dependent on the appreciation, preservation, and affirmation of other people's humanness and humanity (Eze, 2006, p. 79). To become a person involves a proactive participation and engagement of individuals in realising their communities' good (Eze, p. 80). For an African, participation-in-relationship can be understood as the most essential aspect of a human being's identity (Eze, p. 80).

Former Senegalese president, poet, and philosopher, Léopold Sédar Senghor, has also argued that African society is essentially communal. For him, Africa represents a communion of souls, rather than an aggregate of individuals (Senghor, 1964, p. 49). As far as the African value system is concerned, the reality of the community takes precedence over the reality of the individual. According to Ifeanyi Menkiti, the primacy of the community over the individual has an epistemic consequence. It is thanks to the centrality of the community that the individual has epistemic accessibility to his/her own self (Menkiti, 1984, pp. 171–172; Ntibagirirwa, 2007).

African society attaches more significance to the group than to the individual. It values solidarity more than it does the activities and needs of the individual and it places more stress on the communion of persons than on their autonomy. African society is, furthermore, deeply aware of the fact that our human existence is an existence caught in values. Almost re-echoing Senghor's assessment on what he refers to as "a community society built on values," Sekou Toure describes it even more appropriately in the following manner: "Africa is fundamentally communocratic."

From the above, it seems that any future philosophy of m-learning will need to consider (amongst others) the following critical concerns:

– How may m-learning contribute to and promote interpersonal communion as participation-in-relationship?
– How may m-learning give effect to the anthropological maxim that a person is a person through other persons?
– How may m-learning help to endorse the interests of the community and how may it play its part as far as the appreciation, preservation, and affirmation of other people's humanness and humanity is concerned?

- How may m-learning encourage communal solidarity and how may it affect our understanding of communocracy?
- What impact will the future design and implementation of mobile technology, as well as m-learning praxis, have on our understanding of our human existence as an existence caught in values?

Africa's communocratic, "participation-in-relationship" view of humanness and humanity is reinforced by a unique ontology that is based on an assimilating, integrating, connecting, and reconciling "force," instead of on "being," as in traditional Western ontology.

WESTERN ONTOLOGY VERSUS AFRICAN ONTOLOGY

Whereas for the Western thinker *ontos* ("being") is "that which is" or "the thing insofar as it is," for the majority of Africans, ontos is "that which is force" or "the thing insofar as it is force." For most Africans, force is not a necessary, irreducible attribute of ontos. Instead, the notion "force" takes for them the place that the notion "being" traditionally takes in Western philosophy (Scharding, 1996, p. 52). It is because all ontos is force and exists only because it is force, that the category "force" includes, for Africans, of necessity all "beings": God, men living and departed, animals, plants, and minerals. Since ontos is force, all these "beings" appear to most Africans as forces (Scharding, 1996, p. 52). Hence ontos is inconceivable without it being force or inherently endowed with force. There is thus in-built motion ($\Box$ F = m.a). For most Africans reality is a field of interacting forces, where everyone is a centre of shifting forces – existing, as it were, as part of the different relationships that connect the whole of humanity (Eze, 2006, p. 81). On the one hand, the community acts as a guarantor of an individual person's rights, freedom, and liberty (Eze, p. 83). It acts as a *centrifugal* social force. The individual, on the other hand, acts as guarantor of the survival of the community by advancing its good and preservation, knowing that an injury to one is an injury to all (Eze, p. 83). This represents a powerful *centripetal* social force.

The view adopted by African epistemology is, therefore, that knowledge is (the) understanding of (African) ontology; i.e., the nature of forces and their interaction. True wisdom, hence knowledge, thus lies in ontological knowledge; it is the intelligence of forces, of their hierarchy, their cohesion, their interaction, and their assimilating and integrating powers (Soyinka, 1976, p. 49; Temple, 1969, p. 73). For Africans, this should also be the function of teaching and learning ($\Box$education), namely to accompany towards, to instil and to promote an understanding of the nature of forces and their (cosmic and social) interaction, and their assimilating and integrating powers.

In light of the above, we need to consider the following two critical questions:
- How may we – with regard to m-learning – best utilise the African concept of ontos as "force" in directing communal strength, communocratic energy and the power of solidarity towards the advancement and preservation of the good of the community?

– How may m-learning add to our understanding of the nature of social forces and the way in which their interaction, hierarchy and cohesion can contribute to connecting the whole of humanity?

To help us answer these questions, it is necessary to understand, in the first place, how a Western view of learning may differ from an African view of learning, given the ontological fact that learning is a mode of human existence and being-in-the-world. Secondly, it is necessary to draw attention (amongst others) to the new, emergent emphasis on "ambient" learning in the digital age. In the next two paragraphs, I briefly allude to these issues.

CONTRASTING VIEWS OF LEARNING

Learning finds its origin in human intentionality. It is aimed at knowing the world in which we find ourselves and it is about searching for sense and meaning. As such, it is an original way of life (manner of living) of human beings; it is a potentiality that is inherent to being human: human beings learn because they are human beings; they learn like human beings, they stand open for and are intentionally directed upon their world. A human being learns because (s)he is an initiative-of-relationships (Buytendijk & Langeveld, as cited in Sonnekus & Ferreira, 1998, pp. 97–98). As an original way of life of human beings, learning is also a phenomenon of becoming-human. Because of our will-to-learn, we continue to become all the more human: to be human, a person is obliged to become involved in a process of continued humanisation – a process that is fundamentally linked to learning. As such, learning is carried into effect (in the world) as a function of sense-discovering, significance-attribution, experience and involvement.

The manner in which a learner attributes significance to his/her learning (through educational assistance, explanatory teaching, etc.), coupled with how he/she experiences particular learning situations and the manner in which he/she becomes involved in a particular learning task and perseveres with it until it is successfully accomplished, strengthen the learner's perception of his/her place and role within the larger framework of a person-world relationship (Gendlin, 2006). According to Heidegger, for example, learning (and knowing) is an original mode in which a person finds him-/herself in the world. He links it firstly to *befindlichkeit* – to be situated/"emotionally dispositioned" in the world (Gendlin) and secondly to *verstehen* – which includes that a person finds him-/herself understanding/comprehending in the world (Gendlin). Every act that leads a person towards understanding and insight has a situated/emotionally dispositioned undertone and this situated/emotionally dispositioned undertone is the birth/beginning of learning (Sonnekus & Ferreira, 1998, p. 58).

Despite the fact that learning is an original way of life (manner of living) of us human beings, a Western view of learning nevertheless differs markedly from an African view of learning. Current learning rhetoric in the West is, for example, embedded within the dominant grand-narrative of neo-liberalist, free-market discourse and it is predominantly information driven. Hodgson (2002, p. 241) observes that such rhetoric, particularly when implicitly or explicitly linked to ideas associated with post modernity, not only puts the "ARPI" at the centre of the learning process but also increasingly takes the view that the "ARPI" is responsible for managing and directing his/her own training, updating, and education. The work done by Zimmerman (1990), Shute (1994), Schunk (2000), and Leadbetter (2005) seems to confirm this observation. It validates the claim that learning is increasingly being re-conceived as an individualized, personalized, and learner-centred activity. Sharples (2004a, p. 3), for example, goes one step further. He argues strongly that learning is first and foremost learner-centred and individualised and only then collaborative and situated. In the case of m-learning, Sharples, Taylor, and Vavoula (2005) (amongst others) apply the same insight when they claim that learning is a personal and situated activity, mediated by personal, portable technology.

From the above, it seems that Western scholars typically emphasise the personal, individual character of learning. Conversely, Yoloye (1986, pp. 149–172) claims that for most Africans, learning encompasses a three-pronged process, namely:
- learning for society (where all learning is consciously directed towards the collective fulfilment of the needs of society),
- learning about society (where all learning is consciously aimed at thoroughly familiarising the learner with the characteristics of a communocratic society), and
- learning from society (where all learning is consciously directed towards the utilisation of the available resources in society for the promotion of learning as communal participation-in-relationships).

Evidence for Yoloye's claims can be found in, amongst others, the work of the World Council of Churches (Council of Churches, 1937), as well in the work of authors like Okafor, Emeka, and Akumah (1994) and Adeogun (2006). They all observe that Africans view learning as a lifelong social phenomenon – a social enterprise. Drawing on sets of communitarian rules and resources, African learners reproduce, in their social interaction, the structural notion of learning as a communal process that empowers learners to acquire the society of the past, to take part in the society of the present, and to develop the society of the future. For Africans, individual lives are being structurally determined. For them, learning is the collective influence that the entire social structure of a community brings to bear on the humanisation of an individual, i.e. on the act of accompaniment of an individual towards worthy humanness (Adeogun, 2006). In this regard, African society stipulates learning by doing, learning in and through the group, learning by observing, and learning by imitating as methods of advancing towards worthy humanness (Adeogun). Africa considers learning as a means of cultural transmission, as well as of cultural regeneration (Adeogun). They also consider learning as a collective, public process and not as an individual, personal one, as is the case in the West.

From the above, it is clear that a future philosophy of m-learning will need to take the following critical concerns into account:
- How may the fact that as human beings (as initiatives-of-relationships) we stand open for and are intentionally directed upon our world, influence the future design and implementation of mobile technology (hardware as well as its concomitant software) for m-learning purposes?

- What influence will our understanding of human learning as a phenomenon of continued humanisation have on the future design and implementation of mobile technology (hardware as well as its concomitant software)?
- How may future m-learning praxis contribute to human learning as a function of sense-discovering, significance-attribution, experience, and involvement?
- How may future m-learning praxis contribute to and promote human learning as a collective, public, and lifelong social enterprise geared towards cultural transmission and cultural regeneration?

The fundamental contradiction between the notions of the Western "ARPI," and the African view of individual lives as being communally and communocratically determined, has profound consequences for the manner in which we approach any future philosophy of m-learning.

A NEW, EMERGENT EMPHASIS ON LEARNING IN THE DIGITAL AGE

Recently, a number of researchers have been claiming that mobile communication and computing can potentially enable students to share information, coordinate their tasks, and more broadly, function effectively in collaborative settings. In 2002, Hodgson mentioned in her research that mobile technology – and m-learning in particular – is sure to have a major impact on the development of *collaborative partnerships* and transnational *co-operation agreements* [italics added] (p. 252). Sharples (2004a, p. 12) argues that the advent of mobile technology has quickened the search for collaborative learning environments worldwide. He demonstrates how technology and learning is presently co-evolving and how this development is encouraging links between shared workspaces and mobile learning, team learning and contextualised learning. Barker, Krull, and Mallinson (2005, pp. 1–2) even go so far as to claim that mobile technology such as data-centric handheld computer-communicators is emerging as one of the most promising technologies for supporting learning and particularly collaborative learning scenarios. Sharples, Taylor, and Vavoula (2005) extend this claim when they state that "every era of technology has, to some extent, formed education in its own image" (p. 6). They make a case that m-learning should, in future, become increasingly community-centred: successful learners from a mutually promotive community should share their knowledge and support less able students (p. 3).

These viewpoints are also shared by education philosophers such as Chaves (1999) and Nyíri (2006) and by other researchers like Cole (2000) and Dillon (2004). Besides maintaining (amongst others) that the content and structure of knowledge are essentially shaped by the media through which knowledge is communicated, their recent work tends to focus more and more on m-learning and the totality of interactions between learners and their environments – the complex interactions between mind, action, and environment. They also demonstrate how m-learning may provide a means of establishing how "the weaving together of mind and action, individual and group" may allow us to see how learners are positioned within the possibilities of the actions available to them and what they make of such opportunities (Dillon, p. 148).

Over the past three to four years, the increasing ubiquity of mobile technology has, furthermore, seen a steady shift towards "ambient learning" – a phrase coined by Sharples (2004b). In the UK, m-learning is now increasingly being understood as an encompassing, surrounding, non-directional, distributed, encircling, and contextualised process, supported by the use of data-centric, handheld computer-communicators.

At first glance, it may seem as if this new, emergent emphasis on learning as a shared, collaborative, collective, and interactive group and team-like process is ontologically and epistemologically aligned with the above-mentioned African view of learning. I argue that this is, however, not the case. The literature suggests, instead, that there may be at least three reasons for this relatively recent change of emphasis regarding learning in the West:

– Against the backdrop of the grand-narrative of the now dominant neo-liberalist, free-market discourse, it may be attributed to the encroaching ubiquity of transnationalism, the knowledge economy, and the so-called *Third Way* society.
– Instead of being essentially altruistic (i.e., showing unselfish concern for the welfare of the community), as is the case with an African view of learning, this new, emergent emphasis on learning is essentially self-centred, self-preserving, and self-asserting. Its primary objectives do not seem to include learning for society, learning about society, or even learning from society. Instead, it seems to be engineered ultimately towards serving the personal interests of the "ARPI."
– It has patently more to do with linear progress, competitiveness and performativity for the sake of progress and much less with an overriding, encompassing, surrounding, non-directional, distributed, encircling, and contextualised, sincere "ambient" search for belonging, fellowship, understanding, assimilation, integration, and humanising participation-in-relationship, as is the case with an African view of learning.

From the discussion in this paragraph, the following two critical questions push forward:

– How may future m-learning praxis contribute to the design and implementation of essentially noble, altruistic, collaborative learning environments?
– How may education stakeholders and role-players influence the design and implementation of mobile technology, as well as m-learning praxis, so as to contribute to and promote learning environments that may actively reflect a sincere, lifelong search for belonging, fellowship, understanding, assimilation, integration, and humanising participation-in-relationship?

CONCLUSION

The development of a plausible philosophy of m-learning has been hampered, firstly, by the failure of the available scholarly literature to demonstrate convincingly how basic philosophic-anthropological categories may add value to our understanding of the link between mobile technology and human learning. The panoptic influence of teenage civilian journalism and the discouraging observation that our learners are increasingly growing up in an epoch where humanitarian values are decreasing and where a clear vision towards social development is gradually decaying, compel us, however, to reconceptualise and re-narrate issues of "education," "teaching," "learning," "mobility," and "mobile technology" from a philosophic-anthropological point of view.

The development of such a philosophy has furthermore been hampered by the fact that the assembled practices, values, tools, etc. with regard to m-learning are – in practice – still reflecting the perceived wisdom and hidden Western life and worldview assumptions of the predominantly autonomous, rational, possessive, and individualist presuppositions that went into their design.

In order to locate future m-learning praxis within a civilized, compassionate, and caring pedagogy, and in order to actively prevent the crafty spread of an ill-omened kind of Westernised, technological neo-colonialism (as far as m-learning is concerned), it is necessary to consider the possible value that an African life and worldview can add as far as the contemplation of a future philosophy of m-learning is concerned. Not only may a consciousness of an African view of humanness and humanity compel designers of portable digital communicating devices (hardware as well as software) to reassess their enduring fixation on personalisation and individualisation, but it may also urge curriculum designers to investigate avenues through which m-learning may be utilised to inspire a shared communitarian spirit that can result in people being proud of who they are (Metembo, 1996, p. 44).

Applied, integrated competence with regard to African ontology and an African view of learning may compel mobile computer and communication companies in developing countries to investigate ways in which smartphones, PDAs, other portable handheld devices and wireless two-way internet connections may be used in formal and informal m-learning settings to inspire a spirit of self-worth that may help formerly disadvantaged citizens to liberate themselves from the above-mentioned Westernised technological neo-colonialism. Among people of all cultural persuasions, such applied, integrated competence may assist them in using m-learning to foster greater understanding of indigenous knowledge systems. Through the careful selection of relevant curricular content, mobile technology may be utilised to offer learners of school-going age the opportunity of experiencing other cultures and life-styles first hand. Even though such exposure will probably be artificial, at first, (Metembo, 1996, p. 46) the use of m-learning praxis to conscientise people of diverse cultural backgrounds with regard to universal human hardship, poverty, malnutrition, violence, bigotry, racism, etc., can help to sensitise future generations. It can help to make them aware of themselves as social beings who, because of the fact that their existence is an existence "caught in values," should constantly search for and find the meaning of humanness-as-humanisation.

Educationally justifiable m-learning praxis may lead learners to query ways in which interpersonal conflict and differences may be absorbed. The well-planned use of mobile technology in educational settings may promote social justice by guiding learners to explore novel ways of getting rid of their own preconceptions and prejudices. It may contribute to building a social system with common elements to which most people (at least most South Africans) can subscribe.

NOTES

[1] There is some debate on the inclusion of tablet and laptop computers
[2] I acknowledge that talking about the "West" or about "Africa" is, at best of times, risky and invariably suggests a gross generalization. Each of these terms spans an almost incalculable diversity (Van Niekerk, 1996, p. 2). Depending on where the researcher comes from and from which ontological and epistemological perspective (s)he is talking, it is either easy or difficult to answer the question: Does the "West" or "Africa" exist at all?
[3] As in: the general tendency to present myth and metaphor in an idealized human form, midway between undisplaced myth and "realism." Also as in: "a wild-eyed dream of a world state."

REFERENCES

Adeogun, A. O. (2006). *Music education in Nigeria, 1842–2001: Policy and content evaluation, towards a new dispensation.* Unpublished DMus thesis, University of Pretoria, Pretoria, Gauteng, South Africa.

Anderson, T., & Elloumi, F. (2004). *Theory and practice of online learning.* Athabasca, AB, Canada: Athabasca University.

Awoonor, K. (1976). *The breast of the earth.* New York: Anchor Books.

Bandura, A. (2002). Selective moral disengagement in the exercise of moral agency. *Journal of Moral Education, 31*(2), 101–119.

Barker, A., Krull, G., & Mallinson, B. (2005). *A proposed theoretical model for m-learning adoption in developing countries.* Paper delivered at Fourth World Conference on M-Learning, Cape Town, South Africa. Retrieved January 10, 2007, from http://www.mlearn.org.za/CD/papers/Barker.pdf

Becta. (2004). *Becta home page.* Retrieved June 15, 2004, from http://www.becta.org.uk/subsections/foi/documents/technology_and_education_research/ handheld_computers.doc

Belt, H. (2001). *Wireless devices in the classroom. Learning and training innovations.* Retrieved April 1, 2004, from http://www.ltimagazine.com/ltimagazine/article

Berger, J. (2000). *The importance of theory.* Retrieved May 29, 2006, from http://www.suite101/article.cfm/8806/54817

Beute, N. (2004). *Bringing computers and the internet to schools in disadvantaged areas in South Africa.* Retrieved April 5, 2004, from http://www.citte.ac.za

Boote, D. N., & Beile, P. (2006). On literature reviews of, and for, educational research: A response to the critique by James Maxwell. *Educational Researcher, 35*(9), 32–35.

Bowles, S., & Gintis, H. (1976). *Schooling in capitalist America.* London: Routledge and Kegan Paul.

Broodryk, J. (2002). *Ubuntu: Life lessons from Africa.* Pretoria, South Africa: Ubuntu School of Philosophy.

Broodryk, J. (2004). *Oeboentoe sê Afrika sê.* Pretoria, South Africa: Ubuntu School of Philosophy.

Chang, C. Y., Sheu, J. P., & Chan, T. W. (2003). Concept and design of ad hoc and mobile classrooms. *Journal of Computer Assisted Learning, 19*(3), 336–346.

Chaves, E. O. C. (1999). *Technology in education.* Retrieved January 10, 2007, from http://www.vusst.hr/ENCYCLOPAEDIA/technology.htm

Clough, G. (2005). *Informal learning, PDAs and mobile phones.* Unpublished MSc thesis, Open University, Milton Keynes, United Kingdom.

Cole, R. A. (2000). *Issues in web-based pedagogy: A critical primer.* Westport, CT: Greenwood Press.

Council of Churches. (1937). *The churches survey their task.* London: Oxford University Press.

Curtis, M., Luchini, K., Bobrowsky, B., Quintana, C., & Soloway, E. (2002). Handheld use in K-12: A descriptive account. *Proceedings of the IEEE International Workshop on Wireless and Mobile Technologies in Education.* Los Alamitos, CA.

Danesh, A., Inkpen, K., Lau, F., Shu, K., Booth, K., & Geney, D. (2001). Designing a collaborative activity for a palm handheld computer. *Proceedings of CHI, Conference on Human Factors in Computing Systems.* Seattle, WA.

Devaney, L. (2007). "Augmented reality" helps kids learn: Research project uses handheld computers to teach kids math and literacy skills. *eSchool News Online*. Retrieved January 31, 2008, from http://www.eschoolnews.com/news/showStoryts.cfm?ArticleID=6817

Dillon, P. (2004). Trajectories and tensions in the theory of information and communication technology in education. *British Journal of Educational Studies, 52*(2), 138–150.

Draft White Paper on e-Education. (2003). *Transforming learning and teaching through ICT*. Retrieved June 1, 2008, from http://www.info.gov.za/whitepapers/2003/e-education.pdf

Engeström, Y. (2003). *Center for activity theory and developmental work research*. Retrieved January 8, 2007, from http://www.edu.helsinki.fi/activity/pages/chatanddwr/activitysystem/

eSchoolNews Online. (2007). *States seek laws to curb eBullying: Legislative efforts pit online safety against free-speech rights*. Retrieved February 23, 2008, from http://www.eschoolnews.com/news/pfshowStory.cfm?ArticleID=6878

Eze, M. O. (2006). *Ubuntu: A communitarian response to liberal individualism?* Unpublished MEd thesis, University of Pretoria, Pretoria, Gauteng, South Africa.

Gendlin, E. T. (2006). Befindlichkeit: Heidegger and the philosophy of psychology. *Review of Existential Psychology & Psychiatry: Heidgger and Psychology, 16*(1–3). Retrieved February 8, 2006, from http://www.focusing.org/gendlin_befindlichkeit.html#1

Hodgson, V. E. (2002). The European Union and e-learning: An examination of rhetoric, theory and practice. *Journal of Computer Assisted Learning, 18*, 240–252.

Juniu, S. (2003). Implementing wireless technology in the classroom: The iPAQ project. *College Planning and Management, 6*(10), 38–40.

K12 Handhelds. (2004). *K12 Handhelds classroom solutions*. Retrieved June 16, 2004, from http://www.k12handhelds.com

Keegan, D. (2003). *The future of learning: From eLearning to m-learning*. Hagen, Germany: FernUniversität.

Laouris, Y. (2003, November). *An educationally-relevant definition of the learning brain*. Paper presented at the 54th annual IDA conference, San Diego, CA.

Laouris, Y., & Eteokleous, N. (2005). W*e need an educationally relevant definition of mobile learning*. Paper presented at the 4th mLearn World Conference on m-Learning, Cape Town, South Africa. Retrieved January 23, 2007, from http://www.mlearn.org.za/CD/papers/Laouris%20&%20Eteokleous.pdf

Leadbetter, C. (2005). *Learning about personalisation: How can we put the learner at the heart of the education system*. Retrieved June 25, 2005, from http://www.standards.dfes.gov.uk/innovation-unit/pdf/Learningaboutpersonalisation.pdf?version=1

Liu, T., Wang, H., Liang, J., Chan, T., Ko, H., & Yang, J. (2003). Wireless and mobile technologies to enhance teaching and learning. *Journal of Computer Assisted Learning, 19*(3), 371–382.

Mazrui, A. A. (1978). *Political values and the educated class in Africa*. Nairobi: Heinemann.

Mbigi, L. (2005). *The spirit of African leadership*. Randburg, South Africa: Knowres.

Menkiti, I. A. (1984). Person and community in African traditional thought. In R. A. Wright (Ed.), *African philosophy* (pp. 171–181). New York: University of America Press.

Mestry, R., Van der Merwe, J. M., & Squelch, J. (2006). Bystander behaviour of school children observing bullying. *SA-eDUC, 3*(2), 46–59.

Metembo, I. A. D. (1996). *The significance of Ubuntu for the school curriculum*. Unpublished MEd thesis, University of Port Elizabeth, Port Elizabeth, South Africa.

Mosley, A. G. (1995). *African philosophy: Selected readings*. Upper Saddle River, NJ: Prentice Hall.

Mphahlele, E. (1972). *Voices in the whirlwind*. London: MacMillan.

Nasseem, Z. 'b. (2007). African heritage and contemporary life: An experience of epistemological change. In A. T. Dalfovo, E. K. M. Beyaraaza, P. Kaboha, J. K. Kigongo, S. A. Mwanahewa, E. Wamala, et al. (Eds.), *The foundations of social life: Ugandan philosophical studies, I*. Retrieved February 5, 2007, from http://www.crvp.org/book/Series02/II-2/chapter_i.htm

Nichols, M. (2003). *Teaching for learning*. Palmerston North, New Zealand: TrainInc.co.nz/Books.

Nkurunziza, D. R. K. (1989). *Bantu philosophy of life in the light of the Christian message: A basis for an African vitalistic theology*. Frankfurt, Germany: Peter Lang.

Ntibagirirwa, S. (2007). A wrong way: From being to having in the African value system. In P. Giddy (Ed.), *Protest and engagement: Philosophy and apartheid at a historically black South African university*. Retrieved February 6, 2007, from http://www.crvp.org/book/Series02/II-7/chapter_v.htm

Nyíri, K. (2002, August). *Towards a philosophy of m-learning*. Paper presented at the IEEE International Workshop on Wireless and Mobile Technologies in Education, Los Alamitos, CA.

Nyíri, K. (2006). *Mobile understanding: The epistemology of ubiquitous communication*. Vienna, Austria: Passagen Verlag.

Oblinger, D. G. (2007). *Listening to what we're seeing*. Retrieved February 20, 2007, from http://www.information-online.com.au/docs/Presentations/info_online_2007_v6-ho.pdf

Ochs, E. (1997). Narrative. In T. A. van Dijk (Ed.), *Handbook of discourse analysis: A multidisciplinary introduction*. London: Sage.

Okafor, R. C., Emeka, L. N., & Akumah, E. (1994). *Nigerian peoples and culture*. Enugu, Nigeria: ESUTH.

Orr, D. (1991). What is education for? Six myths about the foundations of modern education, and six new principles to replace them. *Annals of Earth, 8*(2), 52–65.

Perry, D. (2003). *Handheld computers (PDAs) in schools*. Retrieved April 5, 2004, from http://www.becta.org.uk/research/reports/docs/handhelds.pdf

Prensky, M. (2001). *Digital game-based learning*. New York: McGraw-Hill.

Ramose, M. B. (1999). *African philosophy through Ubuntu*. Harare, Zimbabwe: Mond Books.

Ravenscroft, A. (2001). Designing e-learning interactions in the 21st century: Revisiting and rethinking the role of theory. *European Journal of Education, 36*(2), 133–156.

Roschelle, J. (2003). Unlocking the learning value of wireless mobile devices. *Journal of Computer Assisted Learning, 19*(3), 260–272.

Rush, E. A., & Anyanwu, K. C. (1984). *African philosophy*. Rome, Italy: Catholic Book Agency.

Sartre, J.-P. (1962). *Das sein und das nichts*. Hamburg, Germany: Rowohlt Verlag.

Scanlon, E., Jones, A., & Waycott, J. (2005). Mobile technologies: Prospects for their use in learning in informal science settings. *Journal of Interactive Media in Education*. Retrieved June 1, 2008, from http://jime.open.ac.uk/2005/25/scanlon-2005-25-paper.html

Scharding, M. (1996). *Part nine: The books of the Latter-Day druids*. Retrieved February 5, 2007, from http://orgs.carleton.edu/druids/ARDA/ARDA-09.pdf

Schunk, D. H. (2000). *Learning theories: An educational perspective* (3rd ed.). Upper Saddle River, NJ: Merril.

Senghor, L. S. (1964). *On African socialism*. New York: Mercer Cook.

Sharples, M. (2000). The design of personal mobile technologies for lifelong learning. *Computers and Education, 34*, 177–193.

Sharples, M. (2003). Disruptive devices: Mobile technology for conversational learning. *International Journal of Continuing Engineering Education and Lifelong Learning, 12*(5/6), 504–520.

Sharples, M. (2004a). *Innovative technologies for collaborative learning environments*. Retrieved June 1, 2008, from http://europa.eu.int/information_society/istevent/2004/cf/document.cfm?doc_id=1143

Sharples, M. (2004b, March). *M-learning: Putting the m and the learning together*. PowerPoint presentation presented at the Universities and Colleges Information Systems Association Conference, Manchester, United Kingdom.

Sharples, M. (2005a, April). *Learning as conversation: Transforming education in the mobile age*. Paper presented at Conference on Seeing, Understanding, Learning in the Mobile Age, Budapest, Hungary.

Sharples, M. (2005b). *Viewpoint: Re-thinking learning for the mobile age*. Retrieved May 29, 2006 from http://www.noe-kaleidoscope.org/pub/lastnews/default-0-read159-display

Sharples, M., Taylor, J., & Vavoula, G. (2005). *Towards a theory of mobile learning*. Paper presented at the 4th World Conference on M-learning, Cape Town, South Africa. Retrieved January 10, 2007, from www.mlearn.org.za/CD/papers/Sharples.pdf

Shute, V. J. (1994). Learning strategies and learning to learn. In T. Husén & T. N. Postlethwaite (Eds.), *International encyclopedia of education* (2nd ed.). New York: Pergamon Press.

Shutte, A. (1993). *Philosophy for Africa*. Rondebosch, South Africa: UCT Press.

Sonnekus, M. C. H., & Ferreira, G. V. (1998). *Die psigiese lewe van die kind-in-opvoeding.* Stellenbosch, Germany: Universiteits-Uitgewers en –Boekhandelaars (Edms) Bpk.

Soyinka, W. (1976). *Myth, literature and the African world.* London: Cambridge University Press.

Stead, G. (2004). M-learning: Small, engaging and at your leisure. *The Learning Citizen, 8,* 10–13. Retrieved July 17, 2005, from http://www.learningcitizen.net

Taylor, J., Sharples, M., O'Malley, C., Vavoula, G., & Waycott, J. (2006). Towards a task model for mobile learning: A dialectical approach. *International Journal of Learning Technology, 2*(2/3), 138–158.

Temple, P. (1969). *Bantu philosophy.* Paris: Presence Africaine.

Thornton, P., & Houser, C. (2004). Using mobile phones in education. *Proceedings of the IEEE International Workshop on Wireless and Mobile Technologies in Education,* Taiwan, 3.

Tsimitakis, M. (2006, November 30). In age of images, are children actors? *Kathimerini: Greece's International English Language Newspaper.* Retrieved December 1, 2006, from http://www.ekathimerini.com/4dcgi/news/ell__KathiLev&xml/&aspKath/ell.asp?fdate=30/11/2006

Vahey, P., & Crawford, V. (2003). *Learning with handhelds: Findings from classroom research.* Retrieved June 16, 2004, from http://www.intel.com/education/ handhelds/SRI.pdf

Van Niekerk, A. (1996). *Anderkant die Reënboog.* Cape Town, South Africa: Tafelberg.

Watson, D. (2001). Pedagogy before technology: Re-thinking the relationship between ICT and teaching. *Education and Information Technologies, 6*(4), 251–266.

Waycott, J. (2004). *The appropriation of PDAs as learning and workplace tools: An activity theory perspective.* Unpublished Ph D dissertation, Open University, Milton Keynes, United Kingdom.

Westwoord, R., & Linstead, S. (2001). *The language of organisation.* Thousand Oaks, CA: Sage.

Wiredu, K. (1980). *Philosophy and an African culture.* Cambridge: Cambridge University Press.

Wood, K. (2003). *Introduction to mobile learning (m- learning).* Retrieved April 8, 2004, from http://ferl.becta.org.uk/display.cfm?page=65&catid=192&resid=5194&printable=

Yoloye, E. A. (1986). The relevance of educational content to national needs in Africa. *International Review of Education, 32*(2), 149–172.

Zimmerman, B. J. (1990). Self regulated learning and academic achievement: An overview. *Educational Psychologist, 25*(1), 3–17.

Zurita, G., & Nussbaum, M. (2004). Computer supported collaborative learning using wirelessly interconnected handheld computers. *Computers and Education, 42,* 289–314.

Ferdinand J. Potgieter
North-West University
South Africa

XIAOBIN LI, HUANG YUXING, & TANG XIAYUN

6. INFORMATION AND COMMUNICATION TECHNOLOGY IN CHINESE EDUCATION

Its Development and Challenges

INTRODUCTION

China joined the World Trade Organization (WTO) in 2001, which has had a far-reaching impact on Chinese social progress. Its impact on the Chinese education system is also noticeable. With an increased awareness of globalization, Chinese educators realize that they need to have a stronger sense of service to establish the necessary education system to meet the requirements of development. China signed the General Agreement on Trade in Services (GATS) and made promises to open up the market of Chinese education (WTO, 2002). The current Chinese education system has these problems: over-centralized administration, isolated environments, and outdated educational concepts.

The gap in education between China and developed countries is obvious. In 2005 the Chinese combined gross enrolment ratio of primary, secondary, and tertiary schools was 69, compared with the US ratio of 93, the Japanese ratio of 86, and the Canadian ratio of 99 (United Nations, 2007). Through international exchange and cooperation, it is possible to introduce into China advanced international practices.

In China, compulsory education is provided from Grade 1 to Grade 9, which is referred to as basic education. Formal education from Grade 10 to Grade 12 is not compulsory, but most youth graduate from secondary school or receive some secondary education (Ministry of Education, October 9, 2007). The increasingly internationalized educational standards are serious challenges to the Chinese basic education system and its curriculum, which we believe is difficult, biased, outdated, and narrow. Too much emphasis is put on the unification in curriculum administration.

Since the opening up policy in the early 1980s, the Chinese economy has changed from a planned economy to a market economy. However, the education system is still quite isolated from the market. Some scholars argue that the Chinese government should allow market forces to play a greater role in education (Dahlman, Zeng, & Wang, 2007; Yan, 2007). Further allowing international and domestic institutions to participate in Chinese education will help to meet people's increasingly varied needs for education.

China made promises of opening up its market in education services, particularly in higher education. The internalization of higher education will be one of the major trends in Chinese education (Ma, 2007), as internationalization of higher education is gaining ground in the world. At the Global Higher Education Forum held in Kuala Lumpur, Malaysia, November 2007, the keynote speaker discussed globalization

T. Di Petta (Ed.), The Emperor's New Computer: ICT, Teachers and Teaching, 77–87.

and what it meant for higher education. In the first plenary session of the Forum, the role of information and communication technology (ICT) in higher education was an important issue for discussion.

In 2003 the Chinese State Council promulgated *The Regulation of the People's Republic of China on Chinese-Foreign Cooperation in Running Schools*. This regulation states that the national government encourages the introduction into China of quality international education institutions to establish cooperation with Chinese counterparts. Currently there are over three hundred cooperative institutions and programs between Chinese higher education institutions and Western counterparts (Ministry of Education, July 23, 2008). These Chinese institutions have introduced advanced international experiences into their operation. Changes have occurred in their autonomy, administrative concepts, curriculum, pedagogy and funding. Opening up the Chinese education services will allow Chinese educators to benefit from other countries' resources and experiences. As the interaction between the world and the Chinese education system increases, Chinese educators and administrators strive to make electronic learning available across the country. They also pay more and more attention to mobile learning and ubiquitous learning (Xue, 2007).

INFORMATION AND COMMUNICATION TECHNOLOGY IN BASIC EDUCATION

The development of educational information and communication technology (ICT) is an important indication of a country's educational modernization. Social development in China requires the continuous advancement of ICT application in its education system. According to the Eleventh Education Development Five-Year-Plan Outline, all elementary and secondary schools will have access to the Internet by the year 2010. It is hoped that the enhanced ICT application will assist the modernization of the Chinese basic education system (Ministry of Education, May 18, 2007). The rapid educational ICT progress helps Chinese educators to deal with the challenges brought about by the fast social change in the country.

In reforming the Chinese basic education system, curriculum reform is the key. Education ICT is a catalyst in this reform. With the advancement of education ICT, the application of multi-media computers and the Internet is increasing in classrooms, which is conducive to a comprehensive curriculum reform.

We believe ICT application facilitates and supports curriculum reform in the following areas:
– Combining ICT application with curriculum materials allows teachers to make teaching and learning more effective and better achieve their curriculum goals.
– Using ICT allows teachers to individualize teaching so that students receive more appropriate teaching, which increases their learning.
– With ICT, a new curriculum will pay more attention to resources outside school, which are not available in the traditional curriculum. With multi-media software and textbooks, Internet education programs, and satellite programs, teachers and students can obtain rich information.

– ICT helps to transform the role of teachers, facilitates updating their knowledge, and changes the relationship between teachers and students.

The Chinese are more aware of international economic competition, which ultimately is a competition of people, especially well educated people with creative ability. The most important task of Chinese education is to educate students to develop creative thinking abilities. ICT facilitates the creation of an informationalized learning environment, where learners can develop their information acuteness, a necessary quality of innovative people in a globalized knowledge economy.

ICT helps to break the constraints of environment, time, and space. This advantage helps to develop students' ability in obtaining and using information. With hyper-text and hyper-media, ICT facilitates the understanding and retention of knowledge, assisting students' self-exploration, self-discovery, and self-study.

Chinese educators need to learn from advanced international experiences to contribute to the process of the Chinese economy integrating into the world economy, which entails extensive international information exchange where ICT plays an increasingly important role. Building an education ICT network provides a necessary information exchange platform. Developing the most advanced education ICT is one thing that must be accomplished to narrow the gap between Chinese education and education in developed countries. It is also necessary to make ICT education available in all schools, where students can develop their ability of obtaining and using information with ICT.

The development of basic education in China is still quite inequitable. There is an obvious gap between eastern and western regions, and between urban and rural areas. The increasing use of ICT in education has helped the emergence of new forms of teaching and learning. Distance education can be open to more students, and students have more influence in determining what to learn and how to learn. Teachers and students in less developed areas can share the same resources with students in developed areas. With unbalanced regional incomes, inadequate educational resources, and a huge task of developing human capital, distance education should play a more important role in making the provision of basic education more equitable. On September 3, 2007 at 10 a.m. over 100 million elementary and secondary students participated in a virtual class through the Rural Elementary and Secondary Distance Education Platform, the Chinese Education Television Station, and the Internet (Wu & Song, 2007). This was the first time in Chinese education that so many students took part in activities in one class.

ICT provides an important condition for student-centered studying. Through educational networks, students can individually obtain information on the most recent scientific development and interdisciplinary knowledge from the curricula in internationally well-known institutions. Without the constraints of status, time, space, and institution, distance education provides an ideal venue for everyone who has access to it.

China has about 434,000 elementary and secondary schools with over 200 million students (Ministry of Education, May, 2007). The Internet and distance education networks have covered over 50,000 elementary and secondary schools, establishing a platform where resources can be shared (Guo, 2007). But there are still many schools to be connected. The demand for education hardware and software is the biggest in the world. If Chinese enterprises cannot meet this demand, competitive foreign companies will have an easy time entering China, citing the relevant GATS principles. Chinese entrepreneurs must develop relevant and affordable education ICT products and facilitate the growth of ICT application in Chinese education.

In 1997, the Ministry of Education started a project of experimental schools for the development of educational technology. Over the years these experimental schools have made progress in building an ICT environment and in promoting the application of ICT in teaching and learning. Experimental schools have also made great efforts to create and improve a system where ICT education is available to all students.

Currently, making ICT education available in all schools is the focus of the Ministry of Education. At the end of 2006, in rural areas, there was one computer for every 39 elementary students and one computer for every 19 secondary students (China Education Info, December 2007). In urban areas more computers are available in schools. But there are problems in educational networks. There is a general lack of comprehensive understanding of these networks among teachers and administrators. In building networks, planning and guidance is inadequate. More attention is paid to hardware, not to software and to training on how to use these networks. Some networks are not well maintained and not used effectively. Sometimes there is even a lack of funding for the proper functioning. Quality is not satisfactory, services after sales are inadequate, and expected outcomes are not realized. Most educational networks are not functioning effectively in providing a better curriculum. Most schools with a campus network are still exploring how to use their network. The positive impact from ICT on education is far from what was expected (Guo, 2007; Xian, 2007).

In 2005, investment in educational information and communication technology was 26.87 billion Chinese yuan (about 3.36 billion US dollars). On April 4, 2005, the Ministry of Education announced a plan to establish a system to train ICT teachers and to recognize teachers' ICT education qualifications. This project has greatly improved the application of ICT in schools. The Chinese Education and Research Net and China Education Broadband Satellite Net will be updated and their capacity will be increased. A China Education and Research Grid will be built to strengthen the connection among regional networks.

INFORMATION AND COMMUNICATION TECHNOLOGY IN HIGHER EDUCATION

On November 6, 2003, the presidents of the world's 18 largest universities attended the International Summit of Large Universities in Shanghai, China, an important dialogue between western and Chinese higher education leaders in distance education at the time. These university presidents agreed to establish an international network of open universities and cooperate in six areas: curriculum development, ICT, program offering, acknowledgement of each other's degrees, information and experience exchange, and researchers and personnel exchange.

A national distance career education and adult education resource bank will be established, where information will be shared. Over the years various information banks have been established, but quality banks are scarce. There is also the problem of standardization, and sharing learning resources is still difficult. To solve these and other problems, the Ministry of Education has formed an expert panel to provide advice and work on the relevant issues (China Education Info, 2008).

On July 24, 2008, China Internet Network Information Centre reported that about 253 million Chinese had used the Internet as of June 30, 2008. This placed China as the country with the most Internet users in the world. However, only about 19 percent of the Chinese population had used the Internet, which was lower than the world average of 21 percent. When compared with the United States' 72 percent, Japan's 74 percent, and South Korea's 71 percent (Miniwatts Marketing Group, 2008), the gap was even greater. There was also an obvious gap within China between urban areas and rural areas in terms of Internet use. While proportionately Chinese lag behind in using the Internet, the annual increase in the number of Internet users is about 56 percent (China Internet Network Information Centre, 2008). It is expected the number of Chinese Internet users will continue to increase over the next three to five years as rapidly as it did in 2006 and 2007 (China Internet Network Information Center, 2007). As more Chinese go online, the Internet will grow in importance as a venue for distance higher education. According to a report from iResearch Consulting Group (2008), the 2007 network education market is approximately 17.5 billion yuan (about 2.4 billion US dollars).

In 1999, Chinese university educators started distance education in four universities with 2,900 students. In 2006 the Ministry of Education announced the list of 68 universities that received approval from the Ministry to provide degree programs over the Internet. These 68 universities had 5 million students registered in various distance education programs, which cover over 10 disciplines (Liu, Y., 2007). The number of institutions receiving the Ministry approval will increase (Yan, 2007). In addition, with lower per student cost, distance education should play a greater role in promoting education opportunity equity (Zhou, Jiezhen, 2007).

Students are admitted into distance education programs twice a year, in the spring and the fall. Usually these students are admitted after passing one of the three sets of higher education entrance examinations: (a) the national adult higher education entrance examinations, (b) entrance examinations designed by individual institutions themselves, and (c) the national higher education entrance examinations. Institutions have some autonomy in deciding how to admit applicants, and most institutions use two or three methods in recruiting their distance education students.

In 2007 most applicants who tried to enter a distance higher education program received an offer of admission (Zhang, 2007). The admission rate for distance education programs is much higher than the admission rate for regular programs, which in 2007 was about 60 percent (Yang, 2007). Some distance education students study for a degree, but others study for a certificate or diploma. Students in a program for a certificate or diploma are mainly people with a job, and their education is considered continuing education. Through distance education about 1.9

million people had graduated by the end of 2004 (Dahlman, Zeng, & Wang, 2007). Chinese distance education learners can be categorized into five groups:
– secondary school graduates studying for a vocational certificate, usually for two to four years;
– secondary graduates studying for a bachelor's degree, usually for four to eight years;
– vocational education program graduates studying for a bachelor's degree, usually for two to six years;
– bachelor degree holders studying for a second degree, also for two to six years; or
– bachelor degree holders studying for a graduate degree, usually for two to three years.

Distance education has reached 31 provinces, autonomous regions, and municipalities directly under the central government. Most institutions offering distance education courses have flexible programs where students study for credits. Once students accumulate enough credits within a specific time frame, they receive a diploma or degree.

In addition to the Internet, most distance education program providing institutions also use cable television networks and satellite technology. As China Mobile Communications Corporation became the largest wireless carrier in the world and mobile technology is available in more areas, Shanghai TV University is exploring the establishment of a mobile campus (Sun & Chen, 2007). In May 2007 New Oriental Education & Technology Group and Nokia, a leading supplier of mobile and fixed telecom networks, reached an agreement to introduce a mobile learning platform so that learners will be able to use a cellular phone to access and download specific course contents (Shen & Ding, 2007).

CHALLENGES AND RECOMMENDATIONS

In China, distance education is a new phenomenon in need of continuous improvement. While Chinese distance education is developing rapidly, it is not meeting expectations. Some of the problems are described in the following paragraphs.

Chinese distance educators have been learning from international colleagues, but there is not enough summarization and analysis of domestic experiences. There is a lack of high quality research to inform practice. There are few teaching models, most network courses stress content presentation and explanation, and instructors do not pay enough attention to the learning environment. The most often used teaching model is a mere transmission of information. A significant part of distance education content is a direct video broadcasting of instructors' lectures, and there is little or no interaction between instructors and learners, or among learners (Hao, Wang, & Wang, 2008). In recent years there has been some improvement in these areas, and learners have more choices. Still, distance education is mainly a transmission of teaching resources and course content (Huang, 2007).

Although network technology is generally shared and there is an opportunity of cooperation, educators use it at their discretion. A broad national system where educators can exchange and share teaching resources has not been established. Some institutions repeat what others have already done, which is a waste of financial resources. To solve this problem, the Ministry of Education promulgated *The Standards of Education Management Informationalization* in 2003. Over the years progress has been made in this area, still there is much to be accomplished (Liu, D., 2007).

There is a shortage of educators with network teaching experiences. Most network instructors are regular instructors with little knowledge in distance education and little network teaching experiences (Hao, Wang, & Wang, 2008). They have a heavy workload of regular teaching and research and do not spend enough time to meet the needs of distance education learners. When distance education expands quickly, quality is not assured.

Since in distance education learners and instructors do not meet in person, network support services are very important. However, there is a lack of guidance provided to learners. Few learners receive feedback on their work from their instructors, and there is little individualized teaching. In designing course materials, instructors tend to emphasize content, but not support (Hao, Wang, & Wang, 2008). In addition, sometimes fees are too expensive, networks are not always stable, and people have misconceptions about distance education.

Since 2004, students who study some general courses through distance education have to take standardized national examinations. These standardized examinations are necessary in improving the quality of distance education programs, and the Ministry of Education has established a national Internet registration system, acknowledging all successful distance education graduates (Li, 2007).

According to one study by the World Bank, the Chinese population from preschool to tertiary level is nearly 260 million, and the labor force of 750 million needs to upgrade its skills (Dahlman, Zeng, & Wang, 2007). Combined, the Chinese population that needs formal education and upgrading skills is over one billion. The education market is huge. The average Chinese education attainment of 8.5 years (Zhou, Ji, 2007) is significantly lower than the 12 years of the Organization of Economic Cooperation and Development countries. Within China, due to the difference in incomes, the gap in education attainment between eastern regions and western regions is wide. The current needs for education expenditures are estimated between 6 to 9 percent of the GDP, but the actual expenditures are about 5 percent, which is low by international standards (Dahlman, Zeng, & Wang, 2007). In 2007, approximately 9.5 million people took the entrance examinations for higher education, among whom only about 5.7 million were admitted (Yang, 2007).

As an important means of life long learning and education for everybody, distance education is developing very fast. With China's huge education needs and geographic dispersion, distance education has great potential. Distance education provides opportunities to different people at various levels in different places. It plays a unique role in building a learning society in China.

In the next three to five years the number of Chinese Internet users will continue to increase rapidly as it did in 2006 and 2007 (China Internet Network Information Center, 2007). By June 2007, over 90 percent of Chinese universities and over 50,000 elementary and secondary schools had campus networks, and a rural distance education network had been established, benefiting over 100 million elementary and secondary students in the central and western regions (Guo, 2007). In November 2006, the Ministry of Science and Technology and the Ministry of Education started the Public Service Demonstration Project for Digital Education, hoping to advance key technologies in providing digital education to the general public, they sought as well to establish a new model of service, providing high quality and individualized digital degree and non-degree programs in order to promote equity and accessibility, and contribute to the establishment of a life long learning system (Yan, 2007). The Ministry of Education estimates that from 2007 to 2050 about 25 to 30 million people per year will need various types of continuous education (Dahlman, Zeng, & Wang, 2007). It is impossible for the traditional means of education to fulfill this task. Distance education should play an important role in meeting this demand.

On June 16, 2007, the Ministry of Education and *China Education Info* journal hosted 2007 Innovation and Development in ICT in Chinese Education Forum in Beijing. At the Forum it was pointed out that while there had been impressive progress in the development of Chinese education ICT, there were still problems (Guo, 2007).

China has the largest radio and TV university system in the world for providing distance education. In the spring of 2007 alone China Central Radio and TV University had 2.24 million students. Even with so much distance delivery capacity, more Chinese students are going abroad to receive education. In addition, more international students are studying in China (Yu, May 29, 2007). Distance education should also contribute to enhancing the world's understanding of China. However, overall most Chinese distance educators have not understood the benefits and challenges of the internationalization of distance education (Ma, 2007). The future of Chinese distance education is bright, but educators and others have to deal with existing problems.

Some distance education programs do not meet students' needs and do not enjoy the reputation traditional programs have (Zhang & Wang, 2007). Since most distance education programs are paid mainly or exclusively by learners, equity is also a serious issue due to the difference in learners' incomes (Huang, 2007). Financial resources lag behind those in developed countries, the level of standardization is low which makes it difficult to share excellent resources, and there are development gaps between different regions (Wang, 2008; Xian, 2007).

On October 27, 2007, International Distance Education Forum was opened in Beijing with over 200 participants. Most participants were Chinese, but there were also participants from Europe, America, Australia, and other Asian countries. The theme of the forum was: Quality and effectiveness of distance education, which are two pressing issues for Chinese distance educators (Song, 2007). To meet the demand of the Chinese economic and social change, to build an informationalized country capable of innovation, and to meet the practical requirements of Chinese education reform and development, Chinese educators and ICT professionals have much to do before China can catch up with developed countries.

To provide quality education with ICT, several recommendations were made. Chinese distance education needs to aim at providing higher education, continuing education, and life long learning opportunities to the masses. Tsinghua University stated that it would focus on providing graduate programs and other high level professional programs. Other universities may consider what they can do to fully utilize their strengths and to contribute to developing education in western China.

Chinese educators need to learn from the practical experiences and theoretical research in developed countries, reflect on their own practice, analyze their own experiences, and construct their own distance education theories (Li, 2007). In those distance education providing universities, programs focused on distance education should be initiated, promoting research on distance education and training distance education instructors to meet learners' needs.

Chinese universities are small societies administered by the central or provincial governments, providing everything to faculty and students. Universities should stop providing services unrelated to learning and focus only on providing learning opportunities and ensuring the quality of learning. Governments should provide adequate funding and monitor the management of universities. Services unrelated to education should be provided by external businesses.

In designing network platforms the interaction among learners, instructors, and administrators needs to be emphasized. Ideally, learners should have an environment where they can freely select courses and receive support. For example, there is a need for a response centre that assists learners in selecting courses and completing assignments.

Finally, to effectively regulate the distance education sector, develop it efficiently and provide equitable opportunities to learners, governments need to invest more in distance education and establish a governance system that facilitates but also monitors the development and operation of distance education programs.

REFERENCES

China Education Info. (2007, December). 农村中小学现代远程教育工程目标将全面实现 [Rural elementary and secondary school distance education project goal will be reached]. *China Education Info, 12*, 3.

China Education Info. (2008). 2007 年中国教育信息化十大事件 [Ten important events in 2007 for Chinese education informationalization]. *China Education Info, 1*, 4–5.

China Internet Network Information Center. (2007). CNNIC 发布《第 20 次中国互联网络发展状况 统计报告》 [CNNIC announces the 20th Chinese Internet development report]. Retrieved November 20, 2007, from http://www.cnnic.net.cn/uploadfiles/pdf/2007/7/18/113918.pdf

China Internet Network Information Center. (2008). CNNIC • 布《第 22 次中国互 • 网 • • 展状况 • • • 告》 [CNNIC announces the 22nd Chinese Internet development report]. Retrieved September 26, 2008, from http://www.cnnic.net.cn/html/Dir/2008/07/23/5233.htm

Dahlman, C., Zeng, D., & Wang, S. (2007). *Enhancing China's competitiveness through lifelong learning*. Retrieved November 10, 2007, from http://web.worldbank.org/WBSITE/EXTERNAL/WBI/WBIPROGRAMS/KFDLP/0,,contentMDK:21387573~menuPK:1727232~pagePK:64156158~piPK:64152884~theSitePK:461198,00.html and http://www.worldbank.org.cn/Chinese/content/Lifelong.pdf

Guo, X. (2007). Speech given at 2007 Innovation and Development in ICT in Chinese Education Forum 2007. *China Education Info, 7*, 3.

Hao, L., Wang, Y., & Wang, Y. (2008). 中英高等网络教育质量保证体系比较与启示 [A comparison of quality safeguard systems in Chinese and British network higher education]. *China Education Info, 1*, 6–11.

Huang, W. (2007). 市场机制引入与远程高等教育公益性的法律保障 [The introduction of market mechanism into distance higher education and the legal safeguard of the public interest]. *Distance Education in China*, August 1, 18–21.

iResearch Consulting Group. (2008). China online education services research report. Retrieved September 26, 2008, from http://www.kinig.com/upfiles/news/20088/1.PDF

Li, J. (2007). 我国远程教育规制的现状及其评价 [An evaluation of the regulations in Chinese distance education]. *Distance Education in China*, July 1, 25–29.

Liu, D. (2007). 总结经验，狠抓重点，进一·推进教育管理信息标准化建设工作 [Summarizing our experiences, becoming more focused, and further promoting the standardization of educational management information]. *China Education Info, 11*, 4–6.

Liu, Y. (2007). Presentation given at 2007 Innovation and Development in ICT in Chinese Education Forum. *China Education Info, 7*, 5.

Ma, L. (2007). 高等教育国际化视域下的电大远程教育：问题与对策 [TV universities and distance education from the perspective of internationalized higher education: Issues and strategies]. *Distance Education in China*, June 1, 31–34.

Ministry of Education. (2007, May). 2006 年全国教育事业发展统计公报 [2006 Chinese education development statistics]. Retrieved November 15, 2007, from http://www.moe.edu.cn/edoas/website18/level3.jsp?tablename=1068&infoid=29052

Ministry of Education. (2007, May 18). 国务院批转教育部国家教育事业发展"十一五"规划纲要的通知 [The state council approves the Eleventh Education Development Five-Year-Plan Outline from the Ministry of Education]. Retrieved September 24, 2007, from http://www.moe.edu.cn/

Ministry of Education. (2007, October 9). 各级教育毛入学率 [Gross enrolment rate of schools by level]. Retrieved February 10, 2008, from http://www.moe.gov.cn/edoas/website18/info33487.htm

Ministry of Education. (2008, July 23). 中外合作办学机构与项目 [Information on Chinese and Foreign Co-Operative Institutes and Programs]. Retrieved September 26, 2008, from http://www.crs.jsj.edu.cn/ article_read.php?id=12-19700101-59

Shen, Y., & Ding, G. (2007). 移动学习在现代远程教育中的应用研究 [The application of mobile learning in contemporary distance education]. *Distance Education Journal, 181*, 37–39.

Song, X. (2007). 2007 年国际远程教育论坛开幕 [2007 International Distance Education Forum opened]. Retrieved November 30, 2007, from http://www.moe.edu.cn/edoas/website18/level3.jsp?tablename=2038&infoid=34553

Sun, Y., & Chen, X. (2007). 开放大学"移动校园"构建的探索 [Exploring the establishment of a mobile campus for an open university]. *China Education Info, 10*, 7–9.

United Nations. (2007). *Human development report 2007/2008*. Retrieved November 28, 2007, from http://hdr.undp.org/en/media/hdr_20072008_en_complete.pdf

Wang, Y. (2008). 我国数字化教育资源现状及发展策略 [Digital education resources and development strategies in China]. *China Education Info, 1*, 9–10.

World Trade Organization. (2002). *Trade in services: The People's Republic of China, schedule of specific commitments* (GATS/SC/135 (02-0796)). Retrieved November 12, 2007, from http://docsonline.wto.org/GEN_highLightParent.asp?qu=&doc=D%3A%2FDDFDOCUMENTS%2FT%2FSCHD%2FGATS%2FDSC%2FSC135%2EDOC%2EHTM&curdoc=9&popTitle=GATS%2FSC%2F135

Wu, J., & Song, Y. (2007, September 4). 一亿中小学生同上一堂课 [One hundred million elementary and secondary students participated in one class]. *People's Daily Overseas Edition*, p. 1.

Xian, L. (2007). Speech given at 2007 Innovation and Development in ICT in Chinese Education Forum 2007. *China Education Info, 7*, 3–4.

Xue, W. (2007). 从 E-learning 到 U-learning [From E-learning to U-learning]. *China Education Info, 12*, 7–9.

Yan, B. (2007). 综观现代远程教育公共服务体系建设 [Establishing a contemporary public distance education service structure]. *Distance Education in China*, August 2, 12–16.

Yang, M. (2007, May 29). 今年高考创下两项新高 [This year's higher education entrance examinations made two new records]. *People's Daily Overseas Edition*, p. 1.

Yu, J. (2007, May 29). 去年来华留学生超过 16 万 [Last year over 160,000 international students studied in China]. *People's Daily Overseas Edition*, p. 1.

Zhang, K. (2007). 试析我国远程开放高等教育办学模式 [An analysis of Chinese open distance higher education models]. *China Education Info, 9*, 15–17.

Zhang, Z., & Wang, Y. (2007). 现代远程教育机构的社会责任 [The social responsibilities of contemporary distance education institutions]. *Distance Education Journal, 181*, 8-13.

Zhou, Ji. (2007, October 17). 坚持教育优先发展，努力办好让人民满意的教育 党的十六大以来教育事业改革发展回顾 [Continuing to develop education as a priority and striving to provide education that satisfies the people: A retrospect at the education reform and development since the Party's sixteenth congress]. Retrieved November 15, 2007, from http://www.moe.edu.cn/edoas/website18/level3.jsp?tablename=2038&infoid=33909

Zhou, Jiezhen. (2007). 现代远程教育—实现我国高等教育公平的砝码 [Contemporary distance education, a tool to realize equity in Chinese higher education]. *Contemporary Distance Education, 113*, 9–13.

Xiaobin Li
Brock University
Canada

Huang Yuxing
Fujian Normal University
China

Tang Xiayun
Fujian Normal University
China

STEPHEN PETRINA, OKSANA BARTOSH, RUTH GUO, & LINDA
STANLEY-WILSON

7. ICT LITERACIES AND POLICIES IN TEACHER EDUCATION

A Survey of Preservice Teachers at the University of British Columbia

Information and communication technologies (ICTs) have intensified and transformed the way we communicate, the way we learn, and the way we teach. They have, we might say, transformed the student and transformed the teacher. However, the convergence of new technologies and education is not entirely positive and unidirectional. Educators and students have had much to do and say about how the new technologies are conceptualized, studied, and used. In schools and universities, for example, educators have oriented ICT initiatives toward instrumentalism, effects, and enhancement (e.g., *How can technology affect or enhance curriculum, instruction, and the training of teachers?*) These types of initiatives fixate on a fallacy that somehow, favorable results will make technology (and by extension, education) look like good investments — technology is just a tool. Instrumentalism reduces technology to neutral objects and processes with specific uses and purposes (Burbules & Callister, 2000, pp. 5–6; Feenberg, 1999; Leidlmair, 1999).

When it comes to technology, most educators are wont to parrot the polemic of the likes of Bill Gates, Microsoft's founder and CEO. Renowned for business acuity and authoritative rhetoric on everything technological, Gates is a master at controlling interpretations of his company and its products. When asked by talk show host Donny Deutsch whether new media were reinforcing crass individuality and anti-social behavior in young people, Gates (2006) spun the question. "Technology is just a tool," he answered, "to let you do what you're interested in…. It's an enabler." Redefining understandings of "social" for the medium, he went on for five minutes explaining how virtual bridge enables him to socialize with his online card game friends every Saturday morning. This type of instrumentalism and technoenthusiasm leaves teachers and teacher educators with few options: vanguard or victim, progress or tradition. Critics of instrumentalism and technoenthusiasm counter with sobering thoughts about lapses of gender, racial, and socioeconomic equity, labor rights, and privacy (e.g., Apple, 1991). Effective technology policy depends on sustained analyses and empirical research into the conditions (e.g., access, commercial control, equity) of technology policies, practices, and literacies (e.g., ideologies, knowledges, modalities) of administrators, designers, students, teachers, and systems managers.

T. Di Petta (Ed.), The Emperor's New Computer: ICT, Teachers and Teaching, 89–109.

This chapter addresses ICT literacies and policies in the University of British Columbia's (UBC) teacher education program. We administered a scale of ICT literacy to students at the beginning and near the end of their 2001-02 and 2003-04 program (N=1,705 pre-program, N=1,173 post-program) (Guo, 2006). We begin by describing ICT policies for teacher education in British Columbia (BC) and exploring the implications for how and what preservice teachers do with and learn about ICTs over the course of their program. We explore the interdependencies between new ICT standards for teachers and the politics of instrumental measures and definitions of ICT literacy. We caution that conventional deficit models simplify interpretations of ICT literacy data. In the final analysis, we note that the UBC teacher education program makes only a slight difference in the students' ICT skills but reinforces instrumental literacies, including perceptions that technology is just a tool. In so doing, we shift emphases from students to policy deficits.

TOOLING UP POLICIES FOR PRACTICE

The phrase "learning technologies" was coined in 1993 when the Association for Learning Technology was established in England, generally as a response to changes in interrelationships between learning and technology, economic imperatives in human resource development, and the waning currency of educational technology (Petrina, et al., 2008). Ben Davis also used the term in 1993, as if by accident, and it remained rare and basically undefined until the mid to late 1990s. Typical of the progress narratives that still characterize the term, Davis wrote that "the sweeping technological advances in learning technologies, now in prototype phase, will be the substantive achievements of the twenty-first century" (p. 21). Reflective of changes in England, the Canadian Office of Learning Technologies (OLT) was created in 1996 to centralize affairs relating to Human Resources Development and the new technologies—to "raise awareness of the opportunities, challenges and benefits of technology-based learning and to act as a catalyst for innovation in the area of technology-enabled learning and skills development" (Canadian OLT, 1998, p. 6). The primary policy directions defined by the OLT included skills development through e-learning and bridging the digital divide (i.e., inequities across class, gender and race). Provincial ministries and universities eventually aligned themselves with funding and policy. For example, the UBC Office of Learning Technology (UBC OLT) was established in 2002 and began to centralize resources on campus, including e-portfolio initiatives. Recognizing the politics of this change, faculties fell in line. In September of 2004, UBC's Faculty of Education (FoE) renamed the Office of Continuing and External Programs to External Programs and Learning Technologies (EPLT). This can be read as both a top down attempt to centralize policy and bottom up alignment with politics.

In the FoE's Mission Statement, "Technology" is one of five emphases underpinning the faculty's research and development mandate. The direction is toward supporting the "development of professional educators who will *use technology to enhance learning* in schools and communities" [italics added]. The technology theme in the Mission Statement derived from the FoE's Technology Task Force assembled in January 2001 and chaired by Dean Rob Tierney (UBC FoE, 2001). The Technology Task Force consisted of 22 faculty, graduate student, library, and staff representatives. The technology policy agenda and direction in the FoE is defined by a series of internally funded projects and administrated through the Dean's Office, EPLT, and Computing and Media Services (CMS). For over four years (2002-2006), the bulk of resources ($732,081 funded) was directed toward funding the purchase of equipment (e.g., laptops), and salaries for CMS systems managers and undergraduate student "Technology Coaches" and "Technology Rangers" for teacher education. As an Associate Dean asserted, the priority was instrumentally "putting technology [i.e., tools] in the hands of students."

The Dean prioritized a policy direction toward *enhancement* of the existing curriculum, or "infusing technologies in teaching and learning in the FoE" (Tierney, 2001, p. 1). This translated into a centralized, discretionary distribution of resources and a model for curriculum and instruction combining systems managers with student Technology Coaches and Rangers that continues through 2007-2008. This specific policy direction and translation into practice were consistent with his work on the Apple Classrooms of Tomorrow project, where students teach technology to themselves and to each other (Tierney, 2000; Tierney, et al., 1992; cf. Robertson, 1998, 2001, 2002). UBC's teacher education curriculum, which excludes technology course requirements, leaves student Technology Coaches, Rangers, and systems managers with the bulk of resources and responsibilities for learning technologies. In 2002-03 and 2003-04, for example, $160,000 in salaries were paid to 150 Technology Coaches to teach and tutor their peers in technology. Systems managers in CMS taught the Technology Coaches about technology. In 2004-05, this practice continued with another $80,000 in teacher education student salaries and benefits and $46,000 for a coordinator. In 2005-06, Technology Coaches were paid from a tuition fund and Rangers were paid from the TLEF. Policy direction, marked by instrumentalism in practice where students and technicians teach technology, emphasizes that technologies are just tools. As we will discuss in another section, when surveyed near the end of their program in 2004, two out of three teacher education students agreed or strongly agreed that ICTs are just tools.

The British Columbia Ministry of Education's (BC MoE) technology policy is invested in similar sentiments. In their *Conditions for Success* report, the BC MoE's (1999) Advisory Committee used the word "tool(s)" 19 times in the 30-page report to describe the use of ICTs in enhancing the existing K-12 curriculum. The policy direction is toward integration and instrumentalism: "Technology should be integrated into curriculum rather than having technology as a separate course" (p. vii). Similarly, in the BC College of Teachers' (2004) *Standards*, a major policy document, technology is mentioned once, in passing, as a resource (p. 15). This policy direction in UBC's FoE, the Ministry of Education, and BC College of Teachers suggests, somewhat naïvely, that technology is merely a resource or tool—students and teachers do not need to study technology (Bryson, Petrina, Braundy, & de Castell, 2003; Carroll & Eifler, 2002; Moll, 2001). Policy for technology in teacher education across BC is nevertheless divided. For example, the

University of Northern British Columbia and University of Victoria require all student teachers to enroll in technology courses while UBC and Simon Fraser University excludes this requirement.

Although there is a range of different technology policy orientations, plans, and requirements across teacher education institutions in Canada and the U.S., policy makers concur over the significance of ICTs. In February 2004, the Canadian Association of Deans of Education convened a symposium to address ICTs in teacher education. The report from the symposium, *Emergent Framework for ICT Integration within Faculties of Education in Canada*, outlines a set of principles that differentiate learning *about* technology from learning *with* technology for teacher education programs. Learning about technology refers to pedagogy dealing with "technical advancements, sociology of impact of technology on students' current and future lives, and the non-neutrality of technology" (i.e., not just a tool) (LaGrange & Foulkes, 2004, p. 7). Learning with technology refers to using ICTs for learning, and modeling the use of ICTs in curriculum and instruction. The *Emergent Framework for ICT* places a policy emphasis on a critical orientation to ICTs as opposed to technoenthusiasm or naïvete (on technonaïvete and ICTs, see Boshier & Onn, 2000; Walker & White, 2002).

For the most part since the early 1980s, policy for technology in teacher education extended from emphases on applications and augmentation to access and the digital divide; from ICT literacy to the integration of ICTs in curriculum and instruction. Computers were introduced into UBC's teacher education program in the fall of 1980 when the BC MoE purchased 100 Apple II Plus microcomputers. BC's early computer literacy theorists, such as Annette Wright, lamented the privileging of applications over implications at this time (1980a, 1980b). For most administrators, teachers, and teacher educators, she said, the emphasis was on instrumentalism or "the technical and mechanistic aspects of computers, to the detriment of their sociological aspects" (1980a, p. 7). Through the 1980s and 1990s, policy makers emphasized augmentation, leaving teachers and teacher educators to puzzle out details of how the existing curriculum could be more efficiently or creatively—the same effect—enhanced. Positive results to this end were nevertheless difficult to find. In 1996, Willis and Mehlinger summarized their comprehensive review of technology in teacher education in one sentence: "Most preservice teachers know very little about effective use of technology in education and leaders believe there is a pressing need to increase substantially the amount and quality of instruction teachers receive about technology" (p. 978). In BC, a survey of the West Vancouver district suggested that teachers were somewhat reluctant and unable to integrate ICT into the K-12 curriculum (Ungerleider, 1997, p. 13; Ungerleider & Burns, 2002). In addition to theoretical frameworks for explaining institutional change (i.e., Fullan, 1982; Goodson, 1988; Hall & Hord, 1987; Hargreaves, 1994, 1997; Holmes, 1991; Siskin, 1994), explanations for the few or slow changes in teacher education included: (a) a crowded curriculum with little time and few opportunities to teach with and about technology, (b) faculty's resistance to the implementation of technology policy, and (c) ambiguous policies on literacies and the lack of technology requirements and standards in certification practices (Bruder, 1988,

1989; Karsenti, Brodeur, Deaudelin, Larose, & Tardif, 2002; Mumtaz, 2000; Willis & Mehlinger, 1996, pp. 981–984). One initiative to correct the policy and standards oversight is the International Society for Technology in Education's (ISTE) *National Educational Technology Standards for Teachers* (*NETS-T*), which correspond to *NETS for Students* (*NETS-S*).

ISTE's (1998, 2000, 2002) *NETS-T* and *NETS-S*, along with the International Technology Education Association's (2000) *Standards for Technological Literacy* are among a long list of current initiatives to establish content and performance standards for educational practice (Kendall & Marzano, 1997; Petrina, 2003). *NETS-T* encompasses six groups of standards:
- Technology operations and concepts,
- Planning and designing learning environments and experiences,
- Teaching, learning, and the curriculum,
- Assessment and evaluation,
- Productivity and professional practice, and
- Social, ethical, legal, and human issues.

Although there are helpful aspects of NETS-T, the emphasis is on instrumentalism or using new tools rather than analysing cultural implications, ethics, and legalities. ICTs are promoted as tools to use rather than capital for reforming workplaces or issues to study. For example, in a seven page article about *NETS*, the word "tool(s)" appears 18 times to describe the use or integration of ICTs in teaching (Thomas & Knezek, 2002). Intent on penetrating practice, ISTE and the National Council for the Accreditation of Teacher Education (NCATE) generated standards for accrediting programs in the United States (ISTE & NCATE, 2002; NCATE, 1997; Northrup & Little, 1996; Waugh, Levin, & Buell, 1999). Policy for teacher education in North America is increasingly performance outcomes and standards-based (Apple, 2001; Beyer, 2002), a scenario underwritten in BC, Coupal (2004) argues, by the neo-liberal government that took office in May 2001. As a response to ISTE's NETS, the BC MoE's (2002a, 2002b) *ICT Standards Guide*, which includes *Getting Started with Integrating ICT: A Guide for Teachers*, represents a policy direction reinforced in the BC College of Teachers' *Standards*. In *Getting Started with Integrating ICT*, the word "tool(s)" appears 75 times in the 41–page standards document reflecting BC College of Teachers', UBC's and ISTE's policy direction for teachers: technology is just a tool. Measurement and norms typically follow standards. The publishing of the Educational Testing Service's (ETS) (2002) *Digital Transformations* signaled ICT literacy as a serious issue of both measurement and policy. The ETS is now in the midst of large-scale assessments and developing norms of ICT literacy in Canada, U.S., and other countries (ETS, 2004; Young, 2004).

DEFINING AND MEASURING ICT LITERACY AND ITS DEFICITS

We initially designed the *UBC Scale of ICT Literacy in Teacher Education* (*UBC ICT LITE Scale*) to evaluate our preservice teachers' competencies, knowledge, and dispositions related to ICTs (Guo, 2006; Guo, Dobson, & Petrina, 2008). We patterned the scale after computer literacy, self-efficacy, and self-evaluation instruments, ISTE's *NETS*, Scheffler and Logan's (1999) rank ordering of computer competencies for teachers, Gibson and Nocente's (1998) survey of FoE students at the University of Alberta (see also Montgomerie & Irvine, 2001), and our local experiences with ICTs. The *UBC ICT LITE Scale* for the pre-program survey in 2001 consisted of 27 items for a self-evaluation of ICT competencies or skills (i.e., none to high degree), 15 items for a Likert rating of the importance of these skills (i.e., not important to very important), 10 Likert items dealing with dispositions toward ICTs in education, and 4 items dealing with technology policy. The post-program instrument repeated most of the items dealing with skills and dispositions, and included the addition of 18 Likert items dealing with the frequency of technology activities experienced in courses and on practicum. The pre-program instrument for 2003 was a near duplicate of the 2001 instrument with a few changes made to items that did not adequately discriminate. We revised the 2002 instrument for the 2004 post-program survey by combining some of the "technology activity" items and rewriting the section of "disposition" items. Again, the goal of the revision was to eliminate some of the items that did not discriminate and to introduce new "knowledge" items informed by critical theories of ICT literacy. We tempered the dominance of items emphasizing "what can or did this student do or expect to do *with* ICTs" (i.e., technology is just a tool) with items addressing "what does this student know *about* certain aspects of ICTs" (technology is political interests). Although we derived the *UBC ICT LITE Scale* from research and experience, we did not adequately theorize the construct we were assessing. We undertheorized the normative component of the scale.

Scales of computer literacy and self-efficacy typically measure a range of literacies, knowledge, and skills (e.g., Albion, 2001; Feng, 1996; Fisher, 1997; Jones & Pearson, 1996; Kellenberger, 1996; Knezek & Christensen, 1996; Medcalf-Davenport, 1998; Oderkirk, 1996; Petrina & Guo, 2007; Ropp, 1999; Willis & Mehlinger, 1996, pp. 1006–1008). Similar to critiques of intelligence tests, computer, digital, information, ICT, or technological literacy (or fluency) are defined by what the scales measure. Constructs such as ICT literacy are nebulous, sliding signifiers but they are *not* meaningless. ICT literacy is a link between action and ideology, and governs a range of economic, educational, political, and social courses of action. As noted earlier, particular expressions of ICT literacy govern policy in BC. One recent attempt to define ICT literacy with precision was made by the ETS (2002): "ICT literacy is using digital technology, communications tools, and/or networks to access, manage, integrate, evaluate, and create information in order to function in a knowledge society" (p. 2). Substitute "knowledge society" for "pedagogical role" and we have a working definition of ICT literacy in teacher education. Similar to the architects of *NETS*, the ETS defines ICT literacy as *functional or instrumental* literacy (see also Committee on Information Technology Literacy, 1999; Eshet-Alkalai, 2004). An antidote to instrumental or neutral models involves re/defining ICT literacy as ideological (Cope & Kalantzis, 2000; de Castell, 1998; Dobson & Willinsky, in press; Ferneding, 2002; Freire, 1970; Graff, 1993; Hawisher & Selfe, 1997, 1999; Kellner, 1998; Kress, 2003; Lankshear & Knobel,

2003; Lankshear & Snyder, 2000; Moll, 2001; Noble, 1984; Peters, 1996; Petrina, 2000, 2007; Reinking, 1997, 1998; Selfe & Hawisher, 2003, 2004; Standish, 1999; Street, 1995; The New London Group, 1996; Voithofer, 2002).

Alternatively, ICT literacy means diversifying applications and meanings of digital technologies from enhancing and reinforcing to questioning and undermining *status quo* practices by exploring new convergences of culture, nature, technology and the self. Substitute "*status quo* practices" with "pedagogically naïve" and we have another definition of ICT literacy in teacher education. Critical judgments on instrumental or neutral models of ICT literacy suggest that there is too much at stake to leave preservice teachers with naïve impressions of ICTs. Lest teacher education be reduced to a practice of show-casing and "Creating Technology Advocates," which is the disposition of too many teacher educators (e.g., Smithey & Hough, 1999, p. 78), we need to question policies and politics that posture technology as just a tool for enhancing curriculum and learning. ICTs have a technical-empirical dimension but they have ecological-natural, ethical-personal, existential-spiritual, and socio-political dimensions as well (Petrina, 2007). As enthusiasts of open source ICTs note, the politics of these technologies are inherently tied to their uses; the five dimensions of ICTs are multifaceted and interrelated. Preservice teachers ought to be educated *with* or *through*, and sometimes *for* technology, but should be educated *about* and *against* ICTs as well. Of course, by working with constructs such as ICT literacy we risk emphasizing individual or psychological dimensions over collective or social dimensions. We risk basing normative judgments on deficit models and limiting ICT literacy to properties of individuals (Fourez, 1997; Roth & Lee, 2002).

Although (teacher) education is normative by definition, deficit models have limitations. For example, anti-racist, feminist, Marxist, postcolonial, and queer theorists detail the problems of educating students in heteronormative, privileged, white institutions. Identifying and filling up cognitive or disciplinary deficits can be a damaging practice. In science and technology studies, researchers found that measures of scientific and technological literacy were used to justify increases in resources for science and technology (e.g., Bak, 2001; Irwin & Wynne, 1996). Deficits in scientific and technological literacy also justified increases of resources for putting a positive spin on controversial issues, such as biotechnology and nuclear power, to counter "ignorance." Currently, with research suggesting that little has changed in uses of ICTs in public school classrooms and academic achievement over the past twenty years, despite billions of dollars of investments and lucrative partnerships for corporate vendors, administrators and investors are searching for easy scapegoats (Barron, Kemker, Harmes, & Kalaydijian, 2003; Farenga & Joyce, 2001; Landry, 2002; Maddux & Cummings, 2004; Muir-Herzig, 2004; Pepi & Scheurman, 1996; Petrina, 2002; Robertson, 2002; Ungerleider & Burns, 2002; Walsh, 1999; Waxman, 2004; Willis & Mehlinger, 1996; Zhao & Frank, 2003). Blame is placed on classrooms instead of boardrooms, on literacies instead of policies. Deficits of ICT literacy become justifications for more of the same policy, more ICT resources, and more revenues for corporate vendors. Research, interpretation, and policy have to be sophisticated enough to accommodate resistance to the integration of ICTs into classrooms and everyday educational practice.

UBC'S PRESERVICE TEACHERS' ICT LITERACIES

UBC's Faculty of Education offers elementary, middle, and secondary teacher education programs. The elementary program is offered as twelve-month and two-year options. Students enter the program with a degree or transfer into the two-year option after two to three years of university studies. Students specialize in the respective grade levels and at the middle and secondary levels specialize in a single teaching subject or major. For the past five years, an average of 420 students completed the elementary program, 70 completed the middle years program, and 460 completed the secondary program. We administered the UBC ICT LITE questionnaire to the teacher education students in September 2001 and 2003 at the beginning of the academic year. In 2001, 877 students completed the pre-program version and 828 students completed the pre-program instrument in 2003. Post-program instruments were completed in May and June 2002 (N=615) and 2004 (N=558). Students identified themselves by an identification number (ID) in 2001 but we did not ask for IDs in 2003. The first part of the findings is descriptive and primarily deals with demographics, access, and basic and multimedia ICT skills. The second part deals with inferences drawn from statistical comparisons.

Demographically, students in the FoE are diverse across a range of categories. For example, about 24% represented racial minorities (e.g., Afro-Canadians, Arab-Canadians, Asian-Canadians, First Nations, Indo-Canadians and Latin-Canadians) in 2003. The vast majority of students were between 20 and 40 years old but ages range upwards to 60 in 2001 and 2003. The majority of students were female (69% and 73% in 2001 and 2003 respectively). About 83% of elementary program students were female in each year but distribution in the secondary program was more balanced during these years, where 56% were female.

A popular, albeit misleading, indicator of the digital divide (i.e., inequities in ICT access, use, and opportunity) is Internet access. For example, the BC Premier's Technology Council (2002) and the BC MoE (2002a, 2002c) consider access to be the key hurdle to bridging the digital divide and frame this as an infrastructure problem (cf. Boshier, Kolpakova & Kinkhamer, 2004). This logic suggests that the digital divide in BC is the narrowest across Canada with 60% of citizens and over 75% percent of small businesses with access and every public school wired to the World Wide Web (web). In our 2001 survey, 81% indicated that they had Internet access at home, 12.5% had a computer without access, and 6.7% did not have a home computer. In 2003 we rephrased the question to include the type of Internet connection and found that 48% had high-speed access and 4% had wireless. Another 12.5% reported that they had dial-up connections while the remaining 33% reported that they did not have access. A large majority of students (82.6%) access the web from home and 17% rely on computers with web access at the university. Microsoft's Windows Operating System (OS) is used by a majority of students: 85.9% in 2001 and 91.3% in 2003. In 2001, 8% were Macintosh users and in 2003 this dipped to 6.9%. A small percentage (1%) reported that they were Linux OS users. In 2003, 92% had either a desktop workstation or laptop, and 9% had both. The majority of students believe that the university should provide ICTs, access to the web, e-mail accounts, and technical support. About 70% of students (in both years) expected the FoE to provide basic applications and lessons on their use.

Skill acquisition and the development of knowledge about ICTs are more complex and less straightforward than most policy makers would have it. The process of learning (something) about and with ICTs is infused into the practices of all disciplines. We intentionally acquire skills and knowledge in some courses and incidentally in others. And, since ICTs are ubiquitous, meaning they are everywhere in most areas of North America life, we also learn by immersion and interaction. Knowledge about ICTs is shaped by, among other forces, the media, cyberculture, and infrastructure. In 2001 and 2003 combined, 73% of the students noted that they taught themselves their ICT skills, reinforcing the adage that ICTs are just tools. About 45% percent noted that they learned from friends and relatives, and about 25% noted they learned their skills in high school, universities, and workplaces. This latter statistic corresponds to the enrolment of females in ICT courses in high schools and universities and is a factor in our inferential analysis of gender. In 2003, 51% of the students noted that workshops were helpful venues for skill acquisition. In 2001, 75% of the students believed that instructors who teach university courses should be competent ICT users. In 2003 this question was modified to address whether ICTs should be integrated on a regular basis into course instruction and 71% answered positively. In 2001 and 2003 respectively, 66% and 73% of the students agreed that there should be an ICT course requirement in their program. Students who offered comments on this qualified their desires with cautions about an already overloaded curriculum. Those who commented tended to be those motivated to learn more about ICTs but who evaluated themselves to be ICT novices.

Self-efficacy and self-evaluation studies of ICT literacy are coincident with research into the use of ICTs over the past twenty-five years. Rather than test students, researchers ask subjects to self-evaluate their level of ICT skill acquisition along a continuum (e.g., none, low, medium, or high), which is the method we adopted. These levels correspond to novice, competent, proficient or expert levels of competency or skill acquisition. The pre-program instrument included 27 skill-acquisition items and 15 items for rating the importance of selected ICT skills (i.e., not important to very important). Percentages of students reporting medium or high levels of skills for modifying word processing documents included 96% and 93% for 2001 and 2003, for creating spreadsheets (60% and 47% for 2001 and 2003), creating a chart or graph (56% and 51%), and using database software (35% and 33%). In 2001, 34% and in 2003, 40% of the students reported medium or high skill levels in creating a presentation (e.g., PowerPoint). In 2003, 57% of students also reported medium or high skill levels in using advanced word processing features (compared to 56% in 2001). Smaller percentages of students reported high skill levels advanced word processing features (24% in 2003) and low percentages of students perceive themselves to be highly proficient in all basic ICT skills. For example, in 2003, 18% who reported high skill levels in word processing also reported high levels in creating a spreadsheet. Only 14% in 2003 felt they had high skill levels in creating spreadsheets and making a chart or a graph. Another 23% felt they were highly skilled in word processing but had no skills in creating presentations.

We addressed a number of skills typically associated with "information fluency," a construct popularized by cybrarians, librarians, and information scientists (e.g., Committee on Information Technology Literacy, 1999; see also Gouzouasis, 2003; Krug, 2004). These include skills for browsing and Boolean searches, downloading and installing applications, and emailing and exchanging information via online discussion groups. Overall, the majority of students reported medium or high skill levels in sending and receiving email with or without attachments. In 2001 and 2003 93% felt that they had medium or high skill levels in using email applications and in receiving and sending attachments. Of the 97% of students indicating medium or high skill levels in using search engines, only 38% felt they had these skill levels for downloading or using images from the web in their projects and documents. In 2001 and 2003, 51% and 56% were moderately or highly competent in installing applications. A vast majority of students are adept at downloading files (56% in 2001 compared to 80% in 2003, perhaps a residue of the mp3 downloading era).

ICTs refer to more than computers, and most workstations are interconnected with a range of devices and peripherals. ICT literacy includes abilities to use and understand the implications of devices such as cameras, media burners, and scanners. Using these devices implies a certain level of knowledge about and skill in image manipulation and multimedia applications. In 2001 and 2003, students reported similar skill levels for using multimedia devices and downloading and manipulating images. Smaller percentages (e.g., 12% in 2003) reported high skill levels in using multimedia devices and manipulating images. Students reported the same skill levels for manipulating audio files and creating music. In 2003, for example, 23% reported that they could manipulate audio files and burn a CD. Nearly three times as many students reported medium or high skill levels in downloading files than uploading files via a File Transfer Protocol (FTP) application. About 25% of the students in both 2001 and 2003 felt moderately or highly skilled in creating a web page and FTPing it to a server. When the students placed a value on basic ICT and multimedia skills they anticipated using in the teacher education program, their ratings corresponded to their skills. Most anticipated using word processing and presentation software most often (2001) or placed the highest values on these skills (2003). Low percentages expected using multimedia skills (2001) and placed relatively low values on these skills (2003).

Similarly, ICTs the students used on practicum or required their students to use were those the student teachers evaluated themselves to be most competent with. For example, word processing and web browsing were the most common ICT activities the student teachers used on practicum. Similar to their appraisal of the FoE's technology support infrastructure, about 39% of the students did not feel that practicum provided adequate support for ICT use or professional development. This reflects Mitchell's (2001) findings of a disconnection between ICT uses in the FoE's Community of Inquiry for Teacher Education (CITE) elementary cohort and those in practicum schools (see also Hare, Howard, & Pope, 2002). The CITE cohort drew on email lists, WebCT, and Hyperstudio but on practicum, students had difficulties finding uses for the ICT knowledge and skills obtained at UBC (see also Krug, et al., 2006). As described earlier, public schools have been disparaged for seemingly inadequate or slow changes with regards to ICTs and the issue is quite complex and controversial. It is questionable whether policy directions (i.e., technology is just a tool) in UBC's FoE and BC's MoE can respond to these complexities and controversies.

We consolidated skill-acquisition items common to the pre- and post-program surveys to create three subscales for inferential statistics. The basic ICT skill subscale was derived from 8 items and the multimedia skill subscale was derived from 5 items. The total ICT skills subscale was a consolidation of the basic and multimedia scales. We converted the Likert items to a point-based scale $(0 - 3)$. A zero meant the student evaluated their skills on the low end. Item scores of 1, 2, and 3 corresponded to low, medium, and high levels of skill. Hence, scores were summed to give an indicator ranging from $0 - 39$ on the total scale, or $0 - 24$ on the basic ICT skill scale and $0 - 15$ on the multimedia skill subscale with a value of reliability of coefficients .96 (Guo, 2006). We employed a series of statistical analyses (i.e., t-test, ANOVA) to test differences between pre- and post-program surveys, age, and gender. We compensated for errors associated with multiple tests on the data set by using .05 alpha or probability levels as a standard for significant differences between groups.

On the total ICT skills subscale, the students' mean scores were higher on the post-program surveys of 2001-02 and 2003-04. In the post-program surveys, students' evaluated themselves to be more skilled in basic ICTs [2001-02: $t(1410) = 2.45, p < .05$; 2003-04: $t(1290) = 2.99, p < .05$]. This was also the case with their self-evaluations on the multimedia skill subscale [2001-02: $t(1490) = 2.72, p < .05$; 2003-04: $t(1271) = 2.60, p < .05$]. The differences are minimal and make generalizations problematic. We hesitate to infer that differences in students' ICT skills over the course of their program are due to anything but attrition or maturity. The majority of the 19% of the students who dropped out of the study could have been those who were unconfident and saw little progress in their ICT skill acquisition. Or program fatigue may have set in. In the pre- and post-program surveys of 2001-02, we asked the students if they felt competent in using technology in a meaningful way but their self-evaluations showed little change between the two points. At the pre-program point 36% did not feel competent and at the post-program point 30% did not feel competent. We regretfully dropped this item from the post-program instrument in 2004. Age differences between students closest to 20 and those closest to 40 years old were significant on the total ICT skills subscale but do not warrant inferences that younger student teachers are more competent or literate than older student teachers with ICTs [2001-02: $F(3, 1355) = 1.27, p > .05$; 2003-04: $F(2, 1220) = 1.59, p > .05$].

In a prior study of participation and performance rates of BC high school students, Bryson, Petrina, Braundy, and de Castell (2003) found that 25% in Grade

11 and 20% in Grade 12 ICT courses are female. However, the females out-perform the males in these courses. Gender and technology interact in complex ways but in the aggregate females are much less likely to participate in formal ICT education and leadership. These differences accrue over time and are evident in UBC's teacher education program. Males had significantly higher mean total ICT skills scores than females in the pre-program surveys [2001-02: $F(1, 1355) = 27.85, p < .05$; 2003-04: $(F(1, 935) = 11.514, p < .05]$. Interaction of gender and time between the pre- and post-program surveys produced a statistically significant difference between pre- and post-program surveys favoring the females $(F(1, 972) = 34.215, p < .05)$. In the aggregate, females show a higher increase than males on the total ICT skills subscale over the course of the program. A randomized sample with equal size groups (female = 702, male = 689), favors females but males total ICT skills scores remain significantly higher $(F(1, 1391) = 65.84, p < .05)$. The mean difference between females and males remains nearly the same between these two points of the program [(female-pre $M = 20.43, SD = 9.71$), (female-post $M = 25.68, SD = 8.87$), (male-pre $M = 25.05, SD = 9.95$), (male-post $M = 29.14, SD = 9.23$)]. In other words, an increase of the females' skills is not enough to offset the difference between the sexes at the start of their programs. The difference remains statistically significant favoring the males. Research on the digital divide suggests that males have advantages (e.g., gender bias and norms in curriculum and instruction, socialization) with ICTs that accrue over time (Bryson, Petrina, Braundy, & de Castell). On the other hand, in self-evaluations of ICT literacy males may be overconfident in their skills.

On average, the students' dispositions toward ICTs on the pre- and post-program surveys are what we might code as positive, technoethusiastic, or ideologically conservative. We nevertheless might be leaping to conclusions here, as the disposition items on the 2001-02 instruments did not differentiate. For example, items that began with "I am interested in learning more" and "I would like to use technology.... [or] multimedia" for this or that made it difficult to disagree. On pre- and post-program surveys of 2001-02 and 2003-04, about 70% of the students agreed or strongly agreed with the statement that "new technologies have a positive effect in transforming instruction." Given a lack of differentiation across the disposition items we dropped or transformed them and added a range of knowledge related to the digital divide and other controversies including labor and online games. Of the 558 students responding to these items, a number reacted passionately and some called them "absurd," "bizarre," "bogus," "gendered," and "sexist," "inappropriate," "impossible to answer," "offensive," "strange," and "opinion, not fact based..." A number of students requested an "I don't know" or "neutral" option for these items. One student wrote that "without reading studies on these statements it is difficult to form an opinion."

These items were intended to help us assess the students' knowledge about ICTs and open a conversation on this aspect of ICT literacy. For the most part, students do

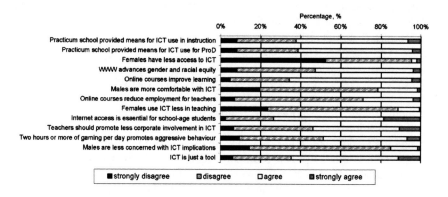

Figure 1. Student dispositions toward and knowledge about ICT issues, 2004

not see gender as an issue for ICT. Less than 5% agreed that females have less access than men to ICTs, 10% agreed that women were less likely to use ICTs in teaching, and 20% agreed that males are more comfortable with ICTs (Figure 1). Another 85% disagreed that males were less concerned with the implications of ICTs than females. A little over half the students agreed that the web advances gender and racial equity. Seventy-seven percent agreed that web access at home was essential for school age students. Responses to these last two items suggest that a majority of students associate the digital divide with access. About 67% agreed that online courses improve the learning process and outcomes for students who are unsuccessful in traditional educational systems and 76% of the students disagreed that online course delivery reduces employment opportunities for teachers. This favorable response contradicts the British Columbia Teachers' Federation's (BCTF, 2000) position which called for a moratorium on the expansion of online courses until a labor policy was in place (see also Petrina, 2005). Online courses in BC grew from a handful of students in the mid 1990s to 14,866 during 2006-07 and labor implications of this growth are unclear. A surplus of about 500 new teachers is created each year from the 2,100 or so part and full time positions available and 2,600 new teacher education graduates in BC (Hawkey, 2006; Petrina, 2008). It is not clear that online courses will provide opportunities for these teachers and seem contradictory given the surplus of teachers in BC. The students were split over whether teachers should advocate less corporate involvement related to ICTs in schools, with a slight edge for those who agreed. We originally included an item about advocacies for Linux but anticipated that the students were unaware of recent trends in open source software. Commercialization of schools through ICTs is a hotly contested issue of politics and rights and the division among the FoE's students reflects the tension (McLaren & Farahmandpur, 2001; Moll, 1997; Robertson, 1998). The BCTF (2000) reported that 25% of BC's schools received corporate donations of ICTs, an increasing trend that is part of larger efforts to commercialize public education in North America (Cook & Petrina, 2005; Molnar, 2004; Petrina, 2006). And as noted, 67% of the students agreed that ICTs were just tools. "Technology," one student wrote, echoing the FoE's policy, "should be viewed simply as an assisting tool for learning."

"ALL JUDGMENTS ARE UP TO YOU"

We should neither feel alarmed nor zealous when, after an entire year of studies in teacher education, a student comments: "I hardly know anything about technology. I'm sure it's a good tool if you know how to use it. But for me it's just a lot of extra work so I do without it." Nor should we feel alarmed when ICTs are dismissed because they are a "headache." But we should be disturbed when a student concludes near the end of a program that "technology is good, but it is just a tool." And we should be impressed when a student volunteers this comment at the beginning of their program:

> In the last fifteen [to] twenty years there has been a great push for the instruction of technology into the classrooms with the vain hopes that a) the technology itself will necessarily improve a teacher's ability to teach; b) the technology itself will be important in the student's life; c) the technology will take care of itself and doesn't need to be used judiciously. None of these are true. Teachers need to understand the appropriate use of technology and the relative unimportance of technologies in students' lives. Teachers need to become aware of technological limitations (current and future) to temper the ongoing push for technology as an answer.

Perhaps we need to begin here, and ask what is the purpose of teacher education (e.g., Britzman, 2003; Cochran-Smith, 2000; Segall, 2001, 2002)? Addressing this question in 2008 requires that we avoid a defense of humanism against the so-called cold rationalities of ICTs. This political move, like technoenthusiasm, reduces technology to instrumentalism: a tool.

In the UBC's FoE, administrators should feel reassured that policies have their parallel in literacies: 67% of students leave the FoE agreeing that ICTs are just tools. However, administrators may be less comfortable knowing that the teacher education program makes only a slight difference in the students' ICT skills or evaluations of their competencies. About 30% of the students said they did not feel competent with ICTs after the program in 2002, and 20% felt they had low levels of ICT skills at the close of the programs in 2002 and 2004. Students' skills increase slightly, albeit insignificantly, over the course of the program, and the digital divide at the beginning of the program remains intact at the end. If policies and literacies are interdependent, they are imperfectly interdependent. The 20% of students whose ICT skills are on the low end may be those 20% who enter the program with either no plans of using ICTs in their future teaching or who do not know whether they want to or not. The teacher education program did not alter the percentage of students with these dispositions. As mentioned earlier, the goal is to shift emphases from students to policy deficits. Can policies (or policy makers) be sophisticated enough to accommodate and even celebrate literacies that are wise to technology and its adherents, critical of ICTs and their promises, or even anti-technology? Can technology policy be formed to make room for Luddites, who were not anti-technology but were critical of certain coordinations and formations of capital?

From 2004 to 2006 in the FoE, nearly three-quarters of a million dollars of external funding was expended on equipment (primarily laptops), Technology Coaches and Rangers (preservice students), and systems managers for the teacher education program. Through these expenditures and similar amounts of internal funds that flow annually into ICTs, policy was redirected in the Foe toward "putting technology in the hands of students." Here, the "technology in the hands of students" includes "tools," practices (e.g., coaches & rangers), literacies, and policies (e.g., instrumentalism). We are now left with the conclusion that "technology is good, but it is just a tool. All judgments are up to you."

REFERENCES

Albion, P. (2001). Some factors in the development of self-efficacy beliefs for computer use among teacher education students. *Journal of Technology and Teacher Education, 9*(3), 321–347.

Apple, M. (1991). The new technology: Is it part of the problem or part of the solution? *Computers in the Schools, 8*(1/2/3), 59–81.

Apple, M. (2001). Markets, standards, teaching and teaching education. *Journal of Teacher Education, 52*(3), 182–195.

Bak, H.-J. (2001). Education and public attitudes toward science: Implications for the "deficit model" of education and support for science and technology. *Social Science Quarterly, 82*(4), 779–795.

Barron, A., Kemker, K., Harmes, C., & Kalaydijian, K. (2003). Large scale research study on technology in K-12 schools: Technology integration and its relation to the national technology standards. *Journal of Research on Technology in Education, 35*(4), 489–507.

Beyer, L. (2002). The politics of standards and the education of teachers. *Teaching Education, 13*(3), 305–316.

Boshier, R., Kolpakova, Y., & Kinkhamer, S. (2004). For internet knowledge, should you ask ol' blue eyes or the brown-eyed girl? *Educational Media International, 41*(2), 117–128.

Boshier, R., & Onn, C. M. (2000). Discursive constructions of web learning and education. *Journal of Distance Education, 15*(2), 1–16.

British Columbia College of Teachers. (2004). *Standards for the education, competence and professional conduct for educators in British Columbia*. Vancouver, BC: Author.

British Columbia Ministry of Education. (1999). *Conditions for success: Report of the Teaching, Learning and Education Technology Advisory Committee to the British Columbia Ministry of Education*. Victoria, BC: Author.

British Columbia Ministry of Education. (2002a). *Getting started with integrating ICT: A guide for teachers*. Victoria, BC: Author.

British Columbia Ministry of Education. (2002b). *ICT standards guide: Response draft*. Victoria, BC: Author.

British Columbia Ministry of Education. (2002c). *Provincial education technology report, 2000/2001*. Victoria, BC: Author.

British Columbia Teachers' Federation. (2000). *BCTF response to the Ministry of Education's Information Technology Plan for 2000 and Beyond*. Vancouver, BC: Author.

Britzman, D. (2003). *Practice makes practice: A critical study of learning to teach*. New York: State University of New York Press.

Bruder, I. (1988). Ed schools: Literacy requirements stagnant, but more offer degrees. *Electronic Learning, 7*, 18–19.

Bruder, I. (1988). Future teachers: Are they prepared? *Electronic Learning, 8*, 32–39.

Bryson, M., Petrina, S., Braundy, M., & de Castell, S. (2003). "Conditions for Success"? Gender in technology-intensive courses in British Columbia secondary schools. *Canadian Journal of Science, Mathematics and Technology Education, 3*(2), 185–193.

Burbules, N. C., & Callister, T. A. (2000). *Watch IT: The risks and promises of information technologies in education.* Boulder, CO: Westview.

Canadian Office of Learning Technologies. (1998). *Professional development and learning technologies.* Retrieved June 1, 2008, from http://www.hrsdc.gc.ca/en/hip/lld/olt/Skills_Development/OLTResearch/Professional_e.pdf

Carroll, J., & Eifler, K. (2002). Servant, master, double-edged sword: Metaphors teachers use to discuss technology. *Journal of Technology and Teacher Education, 10*(2), 235–246.

Cochran-Smith, M. (2000). The future of teacher education: Framing the questions that matter. *Teaching Education, 11*(1), 13–13–30.

Committee on Information Technology Literacy. (1999). *Being fluent with information technology.* Washington, DC: National Academy Press.

Cope, B., & Kalantzis, M. (2000). *Multiliteracies: Literacy, learning and the design of social futures.* New York: Routledge.

Cook, S., & Petrina, S. (2005). Changing tastes: Coca-Cola, water and the commercialization of higher education. *Workplace: A Journal for Academic Labor, 7*(1), 95–111.

Coupal, L. V. (2004). Constructivist learning theory and human capital theory: Shifting political and educational frameworks for teachers' ICT professional development. *British Journal of Educational Technology, 35*(5), 587–596.

Davis, B. (1993). Looking and learning through computers. *Educom Review, 28*(1), 20–25.

de Castell, S. (1998). From data and information to learning and understanding. *Education Canada, 38*(1), 9–19.

Dobson, T., & Willinsky, J. (in press). Digital literacy. In D. Olson & N. Torrence (Eds.), *The Cambridge handbook of literacy.* Cambridge: Cambridge University Press.

Educational Testing Service. (2002). *Digital transformations: A framework for ICT literacy.* Princeton, NJ: Author.

Educational Testing Service. (2004). *ICT literacy assessment.* Princeton, NJ: Author.

Eshet-Alkalai, Y. (2004). Digital literacy: A conceptual framework for survival skills in the digital area. *Journal of Educational Hypermedia and Multimedia, 13*(1), 93–106.

Farenga, S., & Joyce, B. (2001). Hardware versus brainware: Where are technology dollars being invested? *Journal of Technology and Teacher Education, 9*(3), 313–319.

Feenberg, A. (1999). *Questioning technology.* New York: Routledge.

Feng, F. (1996). *The effect of gender, prior experience and learning setting on computer competency.* Unpublished MA thesis, University of British Columbia, Vancouver, British Columbia, Canada.

Ferneding, K. (2002). Stepping through the looking glass: Education within the space between modernity and postmodernity, the lifeworld, the body and technology. *Journal of Curriculum Theorizing, 18*(3), 53–64.

Fisher, M. (1997). Design your future: Technology literacy competency recommendations for K-12 education. *Journal of Technology Systems, 26*(1), 27–34.

Fourez, G. (1997). Scientific and technological literacy as social practice. *Social Studies of Science, 27*(6), 903–936.

Freire, P. (1970). *Pedagogy of the oppressed* (M. B. Ramos, Trans.). New York: Continuum.

Fullan, M. (1982). *The meaning of educational change.* Toronto, ON: Ontario Institute for Studies in Education.

Gates, W. (2006, May 9). Interview. *The Big Idea with Donny Deutsch* [Television series episode]. Eaglewood Cliffs, NJ: Consumer News and Business Channel.

Gibson. S., & Nocente, N. (1998). Addressing instructional technology needs in faculties of education. *Alberta Journal of Educational Research, 44*(3), 320–331.

Goodson, I. (1988). *The making of curriculum.* New York: Falmer Press.

Gouzouasis, P. (2003). The role of the arts in new media and Canadian education for the 21st century. *Education Canada, 41*(2), 20–23.

Graff, H. J. (1993). Literacy, myths, and legacies. *Interchange, 24*(3), 271–286.

Guo, R. (2006). *Information and Communication Technology (ICT) literacy in teacher education: A case study of the University of British Columbia.* Unpublished doctoral dissertation, University of British Columbia, Vancouver, British Columbia, Canada.

Guo, R. X., Dobson, T., & Petrina, S. (2008). Digital natives, digital immigrants: An analysis of age and ICT competency in teacher education. *Journal of Educational Computing Research, 38*(3), 235–254.

Hall, G. E., & Hord, S. M. (1987). *Change in schools: Facilitating the process.* New York: State University of New York Press.

Hare, S., Howard, E., & Pope, M. (2002). Technology integration: Closing the gap between what preservice teachers are taught to do and what they can do. *Journal of Technology and Teacher Education, 10*(2), 191–203.

Hargreaves, A. (1994). *Changing teachers, changing times: Teachers' work and culture in the postmodern age.* New York: Teachers College Press.

Hargreaves, A. (1997). From reform to renewal: A new deal for a new age. In A. Hargreaves & R. Evan (Eds.), *Beyond educational reform: Bringing teachers back in* (pp. 106–125). Philadelphia: Open University Press.

Hawisher, G., & Selfe, C. (Eds.). (1997). *Literacy, technology and society: Confronting the issues.* Upper Saddle River, NJ: Prentice Hall.

Hawisher, G., & Selfe, C. (Eds.). (1999). *Passions, pedagogies and 21st century technologies.* Logan, UT: Utah State University Press.

Hawkey, C. (2006). *Background to teacher supply & demand in British Columbia.* Vancouver, BC: BCTF.

Holmes, M. (1991). Bringing about change in teachers: Rationalistic technology and therapeutic human relations in the subversion of education. *Curriculum Inquiry, 21*(1), 65–90.

International Society for Technology in Education. (1998). *National educational technology standards for students.* Eugene, OR: Author.

International Society for Technology in Education. (2000). *National educational technology standards for teachers.* Eugene, OR: Author.

International Society for Technology in Education. (2002). *National educational technology standards for teachers: Preparing teachers to use technology.* Eugene, OR: Author.

International Society for Technology in Education and National Council for the Accreditation of Teacher Education. (2002). *Educational computing and technology standards for technology facilitation.* Eugene, OR: Author.

International Technology Education Association. (2000). *Standards for technological literacy: Content for the study of technology.* Reston, VA: Author.

Irwin, A., & Wynne, B. (Eds.). (1996). *Misunderstanding science?* Cambridge: Cambridge University Press.

Jones, M., & Pearson, R. (1996). Developing an instrument to measure computer literacy. *Journal of Research on Computing in Education, 29*(1), 17–28.

Karsenti, T., Brodeur, M., Deaudelin, C., Larose, F., & Tardif, M. (2002, April-May). *Integrating ICTs in teacher training: A challenging balance.* Paper presented at the Pan-Canadian Education Research Symposium, Montreal, Quebec, Canada.

Kellenberger, D. (1996). Preservice teachers' perceived computer self-efficacy based on achievement and value beliefs within a motivational framework. *Journal of Research on Computing in Education, 29*(2), 124–140.

Kellner, D. (1998). Multiple literacies and critical pedagogy in a multicultural society. *Educational Theory, 48*(1), 103–122.

Kendall, J. S., & Marzano, R. J. (1997). *Content knowledge: A compendium of standards and benchmarks for K-12 education.* Chicago: Mid-continent Research for Education and Learning.

Knezek, G., & Christensen, R. (1996). *Validating the computer attitude questionnaire.* (ERIC Document Reproduction Service No. ED 398 243)

Kress, G. (2003). *Literacy in the new media age.* New York: Routledge.

Krug, D. (2004). Leadership and research: Reimagining electronic technologies for supporting learning through the visual arts. *Studies in Art Education, 46*(1), 1–5.

Krug, D., et al. (2006). Teacher education students sow seeds of possibility: Teaching and learning with information and communication technologies. *Educational Insights, 10*(2), 6–16.

LaGrange, A., & Foulkes, E. (Eds.). (2004). *Emergent framework for ICT integration within faculties of education in Canada.* Calgary, AB: University of Calgary.

Landry, J. (2002). Is our children learning? *Red Herring.* Retrieved August, 21, 2007, from http://www.redherring.com

Lankshear, C., & Knobel, M. (2003). *New literacies: Changing knowledge and classroom learning.* Philadelphia: Open University Press.

Lankshear, C., & Snyder, I. (with Green, B.). (2000). *Teachers and techno-literacy: Technology and learning in schools.* St. Leonards, NSW, Australia: Allen & Unwin.

Leidlmair, K. (1999). From the philosophy of technology to a theory of media. *Techné, 4*(3), 1–7.

Maddux, C., & Cummings, R. (2004). Fad, fashion, and the weak role of theory and research in information technology in education. *Journal of Technology and Teacher Education, 12*(4), 511–533.

McLaren, P., & Farahmandpur, R. (2001). Teaching against globalization and the new imperialism: Toward a revolutionary pedagogy. *Journal of Teacher Education, 52*(2), 136–1250.

Medcalf-Davenport, N. A. (1998). *Historical and current attitudes toward and uses of educational technology.* (ERIC Document Reproduction Service No. ED 427 721)

Mitchell, J. M. (2001). *Computer technology in teacher education: Tool for communication, medium for inquiry, object of critique.* Unpublished doctoral dissertation, University of British Columbia, Vancouver, British Columbia, Canada.

Moll, M. (Ed.). (1997). *Tech high: Globalization and the future of Canadian education.* Ottawa, ON: Canadian Centre for Policy Alternatives.

Moll, M. (Ed.). (2001). *But it's only a tool: The politics of technology and education reform.* Ottawa, ON: Canadian Centre for Policy Alternatives.

Molnar, A. (2004). *Virtually everywhere: Marketing to children in America's schools.* Tempe, AZ: Arizona State University Educational Policy Studies Laboratory.

Montgomerie, C., & Irvine, V. (2001). Computer skill requirements for new and existing teachers: Implications for policy and practice. *Journal of Teaching & Learning, 1*(1), 43–55.

Muir-Herzig, R. (2004). Technology and its impact on the classroom. *Computers & Education, 42*(2), 111–131.

Mumtaz, S. (2000). Factors affecting teachers' use of information and communications technology: A review of the literature. *Journal of Information Technology for Teachers, 9*(3), 319–341.

National Council for the Accreditation of Teacher Education. (1997). *Technology and the new professional teacher.* Washington, DC: Author.

New London Group, [The]. (1996). A pedagogy of multiliteracies: Designing social futures. *Harvard Educational Review, 66*(1), 60–92.

Noble, D. (1984). Computer literacy and ideology. *Teachers College Record, 85*(4), 602–614.

Northrup, P. T., & Little, W. (1996). Establishing instructional technology benchmarks for teacher education programs. *Journal of Teacher Education, 47*(3), 213–222.

Oderkirk, J. (1996). Computer literacy – a growing requirement. *Education Quarterly Review, 3*(3), 9–28.

Pepi, D., & Scheurman, G. (1996). The emperor's new computer: A critical look at our appetite for computer technology. *Journal of Teacher Education, 47*(3), 229–236.

Peters, M. (1996). Critical literacy and digital texts. *Educational Theory, 46*(1), 51–70.

Petrina, S. (2000). The politics of technological literacy. *International Journal of Technology and Design Education, 10*(2), 181–206.

Petrina, S. (2002). Getting a purchase on "The School of Tomorrow" and its constituent commodities: Histories and historiographies of technologies. *History of Education Quarterly, 42*(1), 75–111.

Petrina, S. (2003). The educational technology is technology education manifesto. *Journal of Technology Education, 15*(1), 63–73.

Petrina, S. (2005). How (and why) digital diploma mills (don't) work: Academic freedom, intellectual property rights and UBC's Master of Educational Technology program. *Workplace: A Journal for Academic Labor, 7*(1), 38–59.

Petrina, S. (2006). Review of school commercialism: From democratic ideal to market commodity. *Teachers College Record.* Retrieved February 1, 2008, from http://www.tcrecord.org/Content. asp?ContentId=12514

Petrina, S. (2007). *Advanced teaching methods for the technology classroom.* Hershey, PA: Information Science.

Petrina, S. (2008). *Observations on hiring trends in the faculty of education.* Unpublished manuscript.

Petrina, S., Castro, J., Feng, F., Hall, L., James, K., Kojima, D., et al. (2008). *On learning and the learning arts, sciences and technologies.* Unpublished manuscript.

Petrina, S., & Guo, R. (2007). Developing a large-scale assessment of technological literacy. In M. Hoepfl & M. Lindstrom (Eds.), *Assessment in technology education* (pp. 157–180). New York: Glencoe-McGraw Hill.

Premier's Technology Council. (2002). *The digital divide in British Columbia.* Victoria, BC: Government of British Columbia.

Reinking, D. (1997). Me and my hypertext: A multiple digression analysis of technology and literacy (sic). *The Reading Teacher, 50*(8), 626–643.

Reinking, D. (1998). Introduction: Synthesizing technological transformations of literacy in a post-typographic world. In D. Reinking, M. C. McKenna, L. D. Labbo, & R. Keifer (Eds.), *Handbook of literacy and technology* (pp. xi–xxx). Mahwah, NJ: Erlbaum.

Robertson, H.-J. (1998). *No more teachers, no more books: The commercialization of Canada's schools.* Toronto, ON: M&S.

Robertson, H.-J. (2001). But it's only a tool: Deconstructing the defense. In M. Moll (Ed.), *But it's only a tool: The politics of technology and education reform* (pp. 14–42). Ottawa, ON: Canadian Centre for Policy Alternatives.

Robertson, H.-J. (2002). Toward a theory of negativity: Teacher education and information and communications technology. *Journal of Teacher Education, 54*(4), 280–296.

Ropp, M. M. (1999). Exploring individual characteristics associated with learning to use computers in preservice teacher education. *Journal of Research on Computing in Education, 31*(4), 402–424.

Roth, W.-M., & Lee, S. (2002). Scientific literacy as collective practice. *Public Understanding of Science, 11*(1), 33–56.

Segall, A. (2001). Re-thinking theory and practice in the preservice teacher education classroom: Teaching to learn from learning to teach. *Teaching Education, 12*(2), 225–242.

Segall, A. (2002). *Disturbing practice: Reading teacher education as text.* New York: Peter Lang.

Selfe, C. L., & Hawisher, G. (2003). A historical look at electronic literacy: Implications for the education of technical communicators. *Journal of Business and Technical Communication, 16*(4), 231–276.

Selfe, C. L., & Hawisher, G. (2004). *Literate lives in the information age.* Mahwah, NJ: Erlbaum.

Siskin, L. S. (1994). *Realms of knowledge: Academic departments in secondary schools.* London: The Falmer Press.

Smithey, M., & Hough, B. (1999). Creating technology advocates: Connecting preservice teachers with technology. *T.H.E. Journal,* March, 78–79.

Standish, P. (1999). Only connect: Computer literacy from Heidegger to cyberfeminism. *Educational Theory, 49*(4), 417–435.

Street, B. V. (1995). *Social literacies: Critical approaches to literacy in development, ethnography, and education.* New York: Longman.

Thomas, L. G., & Knezek, D. (2002). Standards for technology-supported learning environments. *The State Education Standard,* Summer, 14–20.

Tierney, R. (2000). Redefining computer appropriation: A five-year study of ACOT students. In *The Jossey-Bass reader on technology and learning.* San Francisco: Jossey-Bass.

Tierney, R. (2001). *Infusing technologies into teaching and learning in the Faculty of Education* (Teaching and Learning Enhancement Fund Application for Funding, 2002/2003). Vancouver, BC: University of British Columbia.

Tierney, R., Kieffer, R., Stowell, L., Desai, L. E., Whalin, K., & Moss, A. G. (1992). *Computer acquisition: A longitudinal study of the influence of high computer access on students' thinking, learning and interactions.* Cupertino, CA: Apple Computer.

Ungerleider, C. (1997). *West Vancouver teachers' association teacher computer technology use survey.* Unpublished manuscript.

Ungerleider, C., & Burns, T. (2002, April-May). *Information and communication technologies in elementary and secondary education: A state of the art review.* Paper presented at the Pan-Canadian Education Research Symposium, Montreal, Quebec, Canada.

University of British Columbia Faculty of Education (2001). *Technology plan.* Vancouver, BC: Author.

Voithofer, R. (2002) Transgressing digital didactics. *Journal of Curriculum Theorizing, 18*(1), 41–64.

Walker, T., & White, C. (2002). Technorealism: The rhetoric and reality of technology in teacher education. *Journal of Technology and Teacher Education, 10*(1), 63–74.

Walsh, M. (1999). Ka-ching! Businesses cashing in on learning. *Education Week on the Web.* Retrieved June 1, 2008, from http://www.edweek.org

Waugh, M., Levin, J., & Buell, J. (1999). The technology competencies database: Computer support for assessment, teaching, and portfolio management. *Journal of Technology and Teacher Education, 7*(4), 351–363.

Waxman, H. (2004). *A meta-analysis of the effectiveness of teaching and learning with technology on student outcomes.* Retrieved December 2, 2004, from http://www.ncrel.Org/tech/effects2/method.htm

Willis, J. W., & Mehlinger, H. (1996). Information technology and teacher education. In T. Buttery & E. Guyton (Eds.), *Handbook of research on teacher education* (2nd ed., pp. 978–1029). New York: Macmillan.

Wright, A. E. (1980a). *Developing standards and norms for computer literacy.* Victoria, BC: British Columbia Ministry of Education.

Wright, A. E. (1980b). *Microcomputers in the schools: New directions for British Columbia.* Victoria, BC: British Columbia Ministry of Education.

Young, J. (2004, November 12). Testing service to unveil an assessment of computer and information literacy. *Chronicle of Higher Education,* A33.

Zhao, Y., & Frank, K. A. (2003). Factors affecting technology uses in schools: An ecological perspective. *American Educational Research Journal, 40*(4), 807–840.

Stephen Petrina
University of British Columbia
Canada

Oksana Bartosh
University of British Columbia
Canada

Ruth Guo
University of British Columbia
Canada

Linda Stanley-Wilson
University of British Columbia

Canada

Acknowledgement:
We are grateful for the expertise of Judy Paley throughout the duration of the study, and for the expertise of the ICT Literacies Research Team. This research was partially funded by the British Columbia Ministry of Education and the Social Sciences and Humanities Research Council of Canada, Project #410-2006-1679.

TRACEY L. LEACOCK

8. DECISION MAKING PROCESSES AND ICT DECISIONS IN EDUCATION

INTRODUCTION

Enterprise-wide decisions, by definition, have significant impact on the overall well-being of an organization, such as a university. Senior administrators must routinely balance current and future needs, threats, and opportunities. Any significant shift away from the status quo entails many challenges and risks. Unfortunately, the fact that a decision is important and may have far-reaching implications does not mean that university administrators can just unlock the campus crystal ball, peer into the future, and make a decision that will be guaranteed to turn out well. Lower level decision makers, such as department chairs or individual faculty members have even less access to the crystal ball, as they typically have little or no control over the allocation of resources from other areas of the institution, such as centralized technical support services.

There are many reports of attempts to incorporate Information and Communications Technologies (ICTs) into education facing unexpected challenges or failing to meet expectations (e.g., Brzycki & Dudt, 2005; Condie & Livingston, 2007; Hedberg, 2006; Romiszowski, 2004; Wilner & Lee, 2002). In the early days, computer-based educational technologies were touted as cure-alls that would reduce costs, lead to sharing rather than duplication of resources, and enable every student to experience individualized learning instead of the anonymity of large lectures (Bitzer, Lyman, & Easley, 1966; Learning Alliance for Higher Education, 2004; Slack, Morris, van Houweling, & Wishbow, 1984; Wiley, 2000). Yet, not only do traditional lectures persist, when given a choice, many students still opt for face-to-face classes rather than online offerings. The costs have certainly not dwindled, and most professors still rely on traditional published textbooks, supplemented with resources they have created themselves. Some may claim that this means technology-based educational delivery does not work and should be abandoned, but the technologies involved – computers, the Internet, mobile devices, etc. – are too integrated into our society for universities to be able to back away from them and still claim to be preparing graduates for the future. Instead, the focus has shifted to a change in expectations – to the idea of ICTs augmenting, instead of replacing, traditional methods. Yet as long as both hardware capabilities and software options continue to change rapidly, academic decision makers will continue to be bombarded with opportunities to make influential decisions with respect to the uses of ICTs in education, and they will need to make these decisions without certain knowledge of the outcomes.

By looking at research in the field of judgment and decision making (JDM) and considering how it applies to ICT decisions in the academy, this chapter will help

T. Di Petta (Ed.), The Emperor's New Computer: ICT, Teachers and Teaching, 111–124.

administrative and front line decision makers in universities to understand how natural biases in human decision-making processes can influence our "better judgment" and how being aware of these systematic biases can improve the chances of making the decisions that will enable ICTs to have a greater positive influence (and fewer negative impacts) on education in the future.

ICT DECISIONS IN EDUCATION

Academic decision makers know that every action entails some risk, and they generally diligently consider information identified as relevant to try to predict and mitigate those risks as effectively as possible, but this is not the same thing as being able to guarantee the outcomes of decisions. The record shows far too many instances of ICT decisions being made without consideration of critical factors, ranging from ensuring initial buy-in to effective planning for ongoing maintenance and support. Thinkers, such as Bates (2000), have responded to these instances of 20/20 hindsight by developing educational technology-specific guidelines that decision makers can use to build a more comprehensive picture of a situation before making an ICT adoption or continuation decision. For example Bates' SECTIONS model (Bates, 2000, 2005; Bates & Poole, 2003; previously known as ACTIONS) reminds decision makers to consider many key aspects of educational ICT decisions, such as user (student) needs, usability, *all* costs (not just the initial investment), teaching/learning goals and methods, and organizational issues (see Figure 1). The SECTIONS framework is not a comprehensive checklist; rather, it is a guide to prompt discussion of specific considerations as they apply to each decision context, and as such, it can be very useful.

However, such tools do not address more basic questions of how systematic biases in human reasoning processes affect all decision makers, including those making decisions about ICTs in education. These processes will be the focus of the remainder of this chapter.

A BRIEF OVERVIEW OF HUMAN DECISION MAKING RESEARCH

A single chapter does not provide enough space for a thorough review of the vast literature on decision making. Instead, this chapter will present a sampling of some of the key ideas from this literature that may be most revealing to those tasked with making decisions about ICT adoption and implementation in educational institutions. This overview may then serve as a guide to additional readings or as a starting point for discussion.

Two kinds of decisions are of interest in the current context: adoption decisions and progress decisions (Moon, 2001). In adoption decisions, one must decide whether to begin a task, buy a certain product, etc. There are many examples of

S	Students: what is known about the students – or potential students – and the appropriateness of the technology for this particular group or range of students?
E	Ease of use and reliability: how easy is it for both teachers and students to use? How reliable and well tested is the technology?
C	Costs: what is the cost structure of each technology? What is the unit cost per learner?
T	Teaching and learning: what kinds of learning are needed? What instructional approaches will best meet these needs? What are the best technologies for supporting this teaching and learning?
I	Interactivity: what kind of interaction does this technology enable?
O	Organizational issues: What are the organizational requirements and the barriers to be removed before this technology can be used successfully? What changes in organization need to be made?
N	Novelty: how new is this technology?
S	Speed: how quickly can courses be mounted with this technology? How quickly can materials be changed?

Figure 1. SECTIONS model for making decisions about educational technologies (Bates & Poole, 2003, pp. 79–80).

ICT adoption decisions in education, including such decisions as whether to adopt a particular enterprise-wide course management system, whether to purchase (or require students to purchase) laptops for every student in a class, and whether to switch from on-campus labs to online simulations in a first year physics class. Progress decisions, on the other hand, refer to implementation situations. Once the adoption decision has been made, there is work involved in getting everything in place; from there, there are ongoing operations to manage. Both the initial set-up project and the ongoing operations can go well or poorly, and decision makers must monitor the progress and periodically decide whether to continue with the chosen ICT plan or not.

Both adoption and progress decisions, generally, must be made under conditions of incomplete information. By this I mean that there is no way to collect enough information in advance to guarantee the outcome of a chosen course of action. For this reason, such decisions are often referred to examples of as choice under uncertainty.

The Rational Model of Human Decision Making

In the classical, normative view of decision making, people are considered to be rational agents seeking to maximize their subjective utility with each decision.

> The "rational actor" (i.e., the typical person) chooses what options to pursue by assessing the probability of each possible outcome, discerning the utility to be derived from each, and combining these two assessments. The option pursued is the one that offers the optimal combination of probability and utility. (Gilovich & Griffin, 2002, p. 1)

That is, humans weigh all facts, as a computer might, and choose the option with the best overall personal outcome. Any variance from the optimal solution is interpreted as a flaw or error in reasoning that could be repaired with adequate instruction in those of normal intellectual capacity. According to Kahneman and Tversky's description of this model, "It is assumed that all reasonable people would wish to obey the axioms of the theory...and that most people actually do, most of the time" (1979, p. 263).

This very information processing (IP) view predates IP views of cognition by several hundred years. As early as Bernoulli (1738/1954), the view of humans as completely rational decision makers was prevalent. This view also has some intuitive appeal – most people, especially professional decision makers such as managers and administrators, do not think of themselves as making irrational decisions or being influenced by factors that they cannot describe (Kahneman & Lovallo, 1993; Nisbett & Wilson, 1977). It would be comforting to think that every decision about ICTs in education involved accurate assessments of all possible outcomes prior to the objectively defensible "correct" decision being made. However, this is not quite how humans make most decisions most of the time! This is not to say that human decision making is flawed; rather, research shows simply that it often does not follow the cognitively demanding normative approach. For this reason, understanding what people actually do when making decisions is important.

Cracks began to appear in the normative view as researchers started to notice what appeared to be systematic biases in the decisions people make. Groundbreaking work by Kahneman and Tversky (1979; Tversky & Kahneman, 1973, 1974) brought these "exceptions" to the fore and showed that, in fact, the classical, rational model of human reasoning is the exception. Most of the time, people use quite different, more automatic, approaches to decision making. People tend to take shortcuts, they are influenced by affect, and they are influenced by subjective perceptions of gains, losses, and problem frames. Further, when deciding whether to continue with a faltering plan, decision makers are influenced by factors that the rational model predicts should have no impact on decision making, such as feelings of entrapment.

The following sections describe each of these issues in turn and show how they may relate to decisions about ICT use in post-secondary education. However, these descriptions only scratch the surface of the significant literature in each area, thus providing ideas to consider and, I hope, motivation to read more about the fascinating and practical study of judgment and decision making.

Heuristics and Biases

Several researchers (e.g., Kahneman, 2003; Sloman, 2002) have postulated that humans use two systems of reasoning – an associative system that operates rapidly (analogous to our perceptual systems) and a rule-based system that operates more deliberately and effortfully. The more rapid system relies on the automatic activation of heuristics or "rules of thumb" to simplify decision making. It enables us to get by in many of our day to day decisions without too much influence from the more rule-based system. The rule-based system allows us to cross-check automatic decisions and helps us to correct for errors that may have been introduced through hasty use of heuristics. Problems arise when this second system fails to catch an instance in which heuristic reasoning has led to a sub-optimal decision.

According to Kahneman and Tversky's conception, heuristics operate by leading us to automatically substitute easier decisions for more difficult ones (Kahneman & Frederick, 2002, 2005; Tversky & Kahneman, 1974). For example, a broad, complex question such as, "How likely is it that this new technology will improve student outcomes?" is likely to be replaced by an easier question such as, "Would I like to be a student in a course that uses this technology?" The use of such shortcuts is adaptive because, much of the time, the substituted decision will be accurate enough for our needs. However, there are times when heuristics can lead to poor decisions, and decision makers need to be on alert for such situations.

Tversky and Kahneman (1974) initially identified three general purpose cognitive heuristics – availability, representativeness, and anchoring/adjustment, and these are still useful in illustrating the types of systematic cognitive biases that typically influence decision making. More recently, researchers have also begun to investigate affective shortcuts that may have systematic effects on decision making.

Availability

Complex decisions may hinge on a large number of interrelated factors, but explicitly considering every factor and every interrelationship is a cognitively demanding task. Initial work by Tversky and Kahneman (1973; Kahneman, 2003) demonstrated that people tend to work with a subset of all relevant information, specifically that information that is most available. In one classic study, Tversky and Kahneman (1974) asked participants to decide whether there are more English words of at least three letters that begin with the letter "r" or that have "r" as the third letter. Participants were more able to easily generate examples of words that started with r than words that had r as the third letter, and they incorrectly judged that words in the first category were more frequent. According to Tversky and Kahneman, participants substituted the judgment, "How easily can I bring to mind words in each category?" in place of the more difficult judgment, "Which type of word is more frequent?" Thus participants relied on judgments of the subjective availability of relevant information rather than on direct judgments of word frequencies.

More recently, Shwarz and Vaughn (2002) have differentiated between ease of recall and content of information recalled to try to better understand the mechanism underlying the availability heuristic. The availability of examples of successful use of online discussions to promote deep learning can be thought of in terms of, "How *easy* is it for me to think of such examples?" or in terms of, "How *many* such examples can I generate?" In the first case, "availability" equates with ease of retrieval; while, in the second case, availability equates with a judgment of the content that is retrieved. In reviewing published research, Schwarz and Vaughn conclude that people generally rely on the ease with which examples come to mind, unless they have reason to discount this information. In these cases, people will look to the content of the available information and use this as the basis for the decision. Being aware of a natural bias towards putting undue weight on the ease with which something comes to mind and the type of examples that come to mind can help decision makers guard against the effects of over-reliance on this heuristic.

Representativeness

The classic example of an error in reasoning due to use of the representativeness heuristic involves Linda, the feminist bank teller (Tversky & Kahneman, 1983). Participants received a description of a woman that included statements consistent with – or representative of – a feminist, such as, "As a student, she was deeply concerned with issues of discrimination and social justice" (p. 297). They were then asked to rate the likelihood that Linda was (among other possibilities) a bank teller, a feminist, and a feminist bank teller. Logically, regardless of what description one has of Linda, it cannot be *more* probable that she is *both* a bank teller *and* a feminist than that she is a bank teller (only) or that she is a feminist (only). The probability that she is both is, by definition, the product of the two individual probabilities. So, if a participant judged that there was a 20% chance that Linda was a bank teller and a 50% chance that she was a feminist, then, there should be only a 10% chance (.20 x .50) that she was both a feminist and a bank teller. Yet, participants consistently rated it more likely that Linda was a feminist bank teller than that she was only a bank teller. Kahneman and Tversky explain this as the result of making judgments based on representativeness. In other words, rather than considering base rates or formal rules of probability, participants made their judgments based on how much the description of Linda made her look like their idea of a bank teller and how much she looked like their idea of a feminist bank teller.

In the case of ICT decisions in education, availability and representativeness can lead to biased decision making when one unintentionally places too much weight on subjectively available information about a possible course of action. Availability, for example, may lead a decision maker to overestimate the probability of an outcome that is easier to imagine in detail or that the decision maker has spent time thinking through (Sherman, Cialdini, Schwartzman, & Reynolds, 1985). What one finds easier to imagine, in turn, may be influenced by experience. An educator who has recently attended a workshop in which many users of a new technology – such as an online discussion tool – provided glowing examples of how that tool has improved learning at their institutions would likely find it relatively easy to imagine successful outcomes. Another educator who has little or no experience with online discussions, on the other hand, would find the descriptions of effective student activities that used this tool more difficult to imagine (such outcomes would be less available), and such approaches would also tend not to look like (be representative of) what this person thinks good education is. Making a deliberate effort to involve all of the decision makers in generating both positive and negative outcomes of a particular decision will help to make a broader range of possible outcomes more accessible and will also help to bring to light underlying assumptions, such as individual perceptions of what constitutes effective education.

Anchoring and Adjustment

Whether we realize it or not, our judgments are influenced by the first anchor point that we hear on an issue, regardless of the relevance of that anchor to the decision at hand. Although anchoring and adjustment does not fit what has become the classic definition of a heuristic as a process in which an easier decision is substituted for a more difficult one (Kahneman, 2003), it was initially classified as a heuristic and is still an example of reasoning by taking shortcuts – in this case, by overweighting the relevance of initial information. For example, when presented with a proposal to move 15 face-to-face courses to online delivery, the perceived magnitude of this change will vary depending on whether the preamble to the proposal refers to the 1,000 courses on offer at the institution or to a previous initiative to make some other change to the delivery style of two courses. Neither reference provides particularly relevant information to the current decision. Yet, when decision makers anchor on 1,000 courses, 15 can seem like a small number, and when decision makers anchor on two courses 15 becomes a relatively large number (cf. Chapman & Johnson, 2002).

Wilson and Brekke (1994; Wilson, Centerbar, & Brekke, 2002) describe the influence of these anchor points as mental contamination. According to their model, the initial number triggers unwanted mental processing that the decision maker may not even be aware of. Even if one is aware of automatic comparisons between the number given and the current proposal, it may not be possible to correct for the bias.

Anchoring does not have to be tied to simple, numeric information. Kahneman and Lovallo (1993) make the case that decision makers also tend to anchor "on plans and on the most available scenarios" (p. 29). This becomes a problem in that the "best" plan is usually the one that is most susceptible to regression to the mean (i.e., is likely to achieve more typical results than the exceptionally good results forecast). Thus, even if the plan is moderately successful, this is likely to be perceived as a disappointing outcome if the decision makers have anchored their expectations on spectacular success. Kahneman and Lovallo argue that this type of anchoring – and failure to correct – result from using an inside view to assess the situation. When using an inside view, decision makers focus on the unique aspects of the current situation (e.g., "We believe we've got a great team of enthusiastic people" or "We know we were successful in our last project"), at the expense of more general statistical information about the population of similar projects.

Taking an outside view, by looking at success rates and risk factors for similar projects, can lead to much more realistic assessments. Unfortunately, it can be difficult to identify an appropriate outside perspective: "What class should be considered, for example, when a firm [or university] considers the probable costs of an investment in a new technology in an unfamiliar domain?" (Kahneman & Lovallo, 1993, p. 25). Thus anchoring can be both difficult to detect, when one is immersed in a particular decision making context, and even more difficult to overcome. However, making the effort to take an outside view when assessing ICT timelines, costs, and expected outcomes can help decision makers to set realistic expectations and avoid the disappointment and resistance to future ICT projects that can arise when "our" project winds up being just as challenging as the many similar attempts to implement new ICTs at other institutions or in other departments.

Affect Heuristic(s)

Research in the 70s and 80s focused on the role of cognition in decision making. More recently, researchers have begun to investigate the role of affect in decision making (Finucane, Peters, & Slovic, 2003; Loewenstein, Weber, Hsee, & Welch, 2001; Wong & Kwong, 2007; Wong, Yik, & Kwong, 2006). "*Affective valence* is a natural assessment, and therefore a candidate for substitution in the numerous situations in which an affectively loaded response is required" (Kahneman & Frederick, 2002, p. 57; emphasis in original). Affective judgments can occur almost as quickly and effortlessly as perceptions and are another potential source of systematic, heuristic biases in reasoning (Kahneman & Frederick; Slovic, Finucane, Peters, & MacGregor, 2002).

Slovic and colleagues (Slovic et al., 2002) have shown that the perceived risks and perceived benefits associated with a possible decision are negatively correlated. This correlation is interesting because it is entirely possible for an option to have both very positive benefits and very negative risks. Slovic et al. demonstrated that providing information about a perceived risk will increase the negative affect associated with an option, and this, in turn, will decrease the perceived benefits. The reverse holds true when decision makers are provided with information about the benefits of an option. Thus options perceived as good tend to be judged as having high benefits and low risks, and options perceived as bad tend to be judged as having high risks and low benefits – at least in part because of the affect associated with the option.

Schwarz (2002) provides a slightly different interpretation of an affect heuristic – the "how-do-I-feel-about-it?" heuristic. When using this heuristic, decision makers automatically substitute the intuitive judgment, "How do I feel about this?" in place of a more difficult judgment such as, "What will be the impact of diverting funds from the library to provide more on-campus computer labs for students?" Unfortunately, this heuristic can be influenced by such transient factors as the decision maker's overall mood state. The observed correlation between the New York City Stock Exchange and the weather in New York City, for example, has been attributed to the impact of weather on how people feel and the resulting decisions they make (Saunders, 1993).

Loewenstein et al. (2001) provide yet another interpretation of the connection between affect and decision making. In their work on risk-as-feelings, they identify two different ways that emotions can influence decisions. Anticipatory emotions are emotions that the decision maker feels during the decision-making process. Peters and Slovic's (1996) concept of dread (perceived lack of control) is one example of a strong anticipatory emotion that can push decision makers towards being more risk averse than a purely cognitive assessment of the situation would warrant (Loewenstein et al.). Anticipated emotions, on the other hand, refer to one's predictions of how one will feel if this or that outcome comes to pass. Situations with high risks and uncertain benefits are particularly easy to imagine as leading to regret, and it has been well-established that perceptions of future regret can influence the decisions that people make (e.g., Miller & Taylor, 2002).

The introduction of ICTs can result in significant changes in the way an institution or an instructor approaches teaching and learning. This can, quite reasonably, lead to concern over managing resources and ensuring the well-being of students. A decision maker who approaches an ICT decision by first considering benefits is likely to have a more positive affective response and down play the potential risks, compared to another decision maker who approaches the same decision by first considering risks. The different affective judgments are also likely to lead to both different anticipatory emotions and different anticipated emotions, thus resulting in different answers to the question, "How do I feel about this plan?" Yet most decision makers will be unaware of the impacts of affect on their cognitive evaluation of the proposal.

Losses, Gains, and Frames

In addition to investigating shortcuts that may lead to systematic biases in decision making, Kahneman and Tversky (1979) contributed seminal work on the question of what exactly it is that people consider when making decisions. In the classic economic model, decision makers are expected to consider final states – will this or that option put the organization in the best position? However, in introducing prospect theory, Kahneman and Tversky argued that people generally do not make decisions based on end states. Instead, they consider options in terms of potential *change* from the current situation or status quo. Thus every decision becomes a choice among gains and losses, rather than a consideration of best outcomes.

However, people show diminishing sensitivity to the size of these gains and losses (LeBoeuf & Shafir, 2005). For example, the perceived benefit of installing 60 additional computers in on campus computer labs will be less than double the magnitude of the perceived benefit of installing only 30 additional computers. The more computers that are installed, the less each additional computer contributes to the overall perception of value-added.

Another important finding within prospect theory is that the way a choice situation is framed can have a significant impact on the resulting decision (Kahneman & Tversky, 1979; LeBoeuf & Shafir, 2005). More specifically, people tend to be risk-averse when a decision is presented as a choice between positive outcomes and risk-seeking when a decision is presented as a choice between negative outcomes. Consider a scenario in which a department is trying to increase enrolments. The department has decided to open up additional seats by adding a new section in a course that always has a long wait list. The department must decide, however, whether the new section should be online or lecture-based. The curriculum committee is confident in their predictions of enrolment for the lecture option, but they are less certain about what to expect with an online option. Assuming the target enrolment for the course is 150 students, how the two options are framed may affect the committee's choice (see Figure 2). In each case, prospect theory predicts that the starred option will be selected. Notice that if you calculate the expected values of all four options, they are the same (120 students, i.e., 30 short of the target). However, research shows (a) that people will generally express a strong preference for one option over the other within each pair (A-B and C-D), and (b) that this preference can be reversed by changing the frame of reference used to describe the options – in this case, changing between predictions of number of students enrolled and of shortfalls from the target.

In complex, real-world contexts, the status quo itself may be something of a moving target. For example, if an institution predicts that total enrolment will drop 5% over the next five years, then the possibility of reducing the size of this drop to 2% by expanding to new markets through increased online course offerings could be interpreted as a gain over the anticipated status quo, even though there would still be a net decrease in enrolment (Kahneman & Lovallo, 1993).

In summary, the magnitude and direction of changes from the status quo are more salient than the end states themselves, and the way a decision situation is presented or framed can have a surprisingly large impact on which option a decision maker will chose. It can be a valuable exercise for decision makers to consciously reframe decision options in a variety of ways to test whether the best option remains constant across problem frames or whether it is an artifact of a particular way of viewing the situation (Kahneman & Lovallo, 1993).

Positive Frame (anticipated enrolments)

Option A - Lecture: enrolment will be 120 students*

Option B - Online: 1/3 probability that enrolment will be 150 students and 2/3 probability that enrolment will be only 105 students

Negative Frame (anticipated shortfalls)

Option C - Lecture: enrolment will be 30 below the target

Option D - Online: 1/3 chance that enrolment will be 90 below target and 2/3 probability that enrolment will be 150 (on target)*

Figure 2. Example of impact of framing on decisions under uncertainty (adapted from Kahneman & Tversky, 1984).

Escalation of Commitment

Finally, the phenomenon of "escalation of commitment" in ongoing projects (e.g., Garland, 1990; Karlsson, Juliusson, & Gärling, 2005) is also worth mention. In escalation-of-commitment situations, decision-makers involved in an ongoing project must decide whether to continue to invest resources to follow through on an initial plan (escalating the commitment to that plan) or to abandon the current plan and start with a new plan.

There are three features that define the classic escalation of commitment situation (Moon, 2001). First, significant resources, such as time, money, effort, or even reputation, must already have been invested in the original approach. Second, there must be negative feedback associated with the unfinished task; in academic ICT decisions common forms of negative feedback include unexpectedly high costs, slow uptake or outright resistance from users, and unexpected technical barriers. Third, the decision maker must face the decision of continuing with the original plan or abandoning that plan for a new one.

The decision to escalate one's commitment to a course of action in the face of negative feedback has been viewed as an example of entrapment. Entrapment may occur when one has invested significant resources and feels compelled to continue investing more resources in the same plan, even if it now seems that plan will not lead to complete success (Moon, 2001). Rationally, because one cannot recover such sunk costs, they should not factor into decisions people make about how to move forward. Yet, researchers have shown that people often do consider sunk costs when making decisions (e.g., Wong, Yik, & Kwong, 2006). Further, the more one perceives oneself as responsible for those costs, the more of a factor they become in future decisions (Wong, Yik, & Kwong). Bornstein and Chapman (1995) provided evidence that decision makers view changing paths after having made a large investment in one direction as a waste – or as throwing away the initial investment. Because wastefulness is undesirable, particularly in an era of every-increasing accountability requirements, there is pressure to continue along the path paved by the initial investments.

CONCLUSION

The decision making research has not focused on how people make decisions in the context of education, yet much that this literature has to offer can be valuable to those tasked with making large or small decisions about how educational technologies can best facilitate educational goals. This chapter provides a brief tour of some foundational examples of how human decision making processes diverge from our intuitive understanding of ourselves as rational decision makers.

Although there is a natural tendency to believe both that the decisions we make are rational and not influenced by extraneous factors and that we have control over the critical factors that will enable our project to avoid the pitfalls that similar projects have faced, the judgment and decision making literature shows that these assumptions are usually false. Even the most experienced decision makers take short cuts; they allow their emotions to have unexamined influence over decisions; they fall victim to framing effects; and they face the pressures of entrapment. By being aware of the influence of these process, decision makers can be better prepared to examine the real reasons for each decision and differentiate between critical factors and the automatically-processed judgments and interpretations that serve us well much of the time.

REFERENCES

Bates, A. W. (2000). *Managing technological change: Strategies for college and university leaders*. San Francisco, CA: Jossey-Bass.

Bates, A. W. (2005). *Technology, e-learning and distance education* (2nd ed.). New York: Routledge.

Bates, A. W., & Poole, G. (2003). *Effective teaching with technology in higher education*. San Francisco, CA: Jossey-Bass.

Bernoulli, D. (1954). Exposition of a new theory on the measurement of risk. *Econometrica, 22*, 23–36. (Original work published 1738)

Bitzer, D. L., Lyman, E. R., & Easley, J. A. J. (1966, April). *The uses of PLATO: A computer controlled teaching system*. Paper presented at the Proceedings of the 1966 Clinic on Library Applications of Data Processing, Urbana, IL.

Bornstein, B. H., & Chapman, G. B. (1995). Learning lessons from sunk costs. *Journal of Experimental Psychology: Applied, 1*, 251–269.

Brzycki, D., & Dudt, K. (2005). Overcoming barriers to technology use in teacher preparation programs. *Journal of Technology and Teacher Education, 13*(4), 619–641.

Chapman, G. B., & Johnson, E. J. (2002). Incorporating the irrelevant: Anchors in judgments of belief and value. In T. Gilovich, D. Griffin, & D. Kahneman (Eds.), *Heuristics and biases: The psychology of intuitive judgment* (pp. 120–138). New York: Cambridge University Press.

Condie, R., & Livingston, K. (2007). Blending online learning with traditional approaches: Changing practices. *British Journal of Educational Technology, 38*(2), 337–348.

Finucane, M. L., Peters, E., & Slovic, P. (2003). Judgment and decision making: The dance of affect and reason. In S. L. Schneider, & J. Shanteau (Eds.), *Emerging perspectives on judgment and decision research* (pp. 327–346). New York: Cambridge University Press.

Garland, H. (1990). Throwing good money after bad: The effect of sunk costs on the decision to escalate commitment to an ongoing project. *Journal of Applied Psychology, 75*, 728–731.

Gilovich, T., & Griffin, D. (2002). Introduction – heuristics and biases: Then and now. In T. Gilovich, D. Griffin, & D. Kahneman (Eds.), *Heuristics and biases: The psychology of intuitive judgment* (pp. 1–18). New York: Cambridge University Press.

Hedberg, J. G. (2006). E-learning futures? Speculations for a time yet to come. *Studies in Continuing Education, 28*(2), 171–183.

Kahneman, D. (2003). A perspective on judgment and choice: Mapping bounded rationality. *American Psychologist, 58*, 697–720.

Kahneman, D., & Frederick, S. (2002). Representativeness revisited: Attribute substitution in intuitive judgment. In T. Gilovich, D. Griffin, & D. Kahneman (Eds.), *Heuristics and biases: The psychology of intuitive judgment* (pp. 49–81). New York: Cambridge University Press.

Kahneman, D., & Frederick, S. (2005). A model of heuristic judgment. In K. J. Holyoak, & R. G. Morrison (Eds.), *The Cambridge handbook of thinking and reasoning* (pp. 267–293). New York: Cambridge University Press.

Kahneman, D., & Lovallo, D. (1993). Timid choices and bold forecasts: A cognitive perspective of risk taking. *Management Science, 39*(1), 17–31.

Kahneman, D., & Tversky, A. (1979). Prospect theory: An analysis of decisions under risk. *Econometrica, 47*, 263–291.

Kahneman, D., & Tversky, A. (1984). Choices, values, and frames. *American Psychologist, 39*(4), 341–350.

Karlsson, N., Juliusson, E. A., & Gärling, T. (2005). A conceptualization of task dimensions affecting escalation of commitment. *European Journal of Cognitive Psychology, 17*, 835–858.

Learning Alliance for Higher Education. (2004). Mixed skies ahead: What happened to e-learning and why change. *Change*, March/April, 55–58.

LeBoeuf, R. A., & Shafir, E. (2005). Decision making. In K. J. Holyoak, & R. G. Morrison (Eds.), *The Cambridge handbook of thinking and reasoning* (pp. 243–265). New York: Cambridge University Press.

Loewenstein, G. F., Weber, E. U., Hsee, C. K., & Welch, N. (2001). Risk as feelings. *Psychological Bulletin, 127*, 267–286.

Miller, D. T., & Taylor, B. R. (2002). Counterfactual thought, regret, and superstition: How to avoid kicking yourself. In T. Gilovich, D. Griffin, & D. Kahneman (Eds.), *Heuristics and biases: The psychology of intuitive judgment* (pp. 367–378). New York: Cambridge University Press.

Moon, H. (2001). Looking forward and looking back: Integrating completion and sunk-cost effects within an escalation-of-commitment progress decision. *Journal of Applied Psychology, 86*(1), 104–113.

Nisbett, R. E., & Wilson, T. D. (1977). Telling more than we can know: Verbal reports on mental processes. *Psychological Review, 84*, 231–259.

Peters, E., & Slovic, P. (1996). The role of affect and worldviews as orienting dispositions in the perception and acceptance of nuclear power. *Journal of Applied Social Psychology, 26*, 1427–1453.

Romiszowski, A. (2004). How's the e-learning baby? Factors leading to success or failure of an educational technology innovation. *Educational Technology, 44*(1), 5–27.

Saunders, E. M., Jr. (1993). Stock prices and Wall Street weather. *American Economic Review, 83*, 1337–1345.

Schwarz, N. (2002). Feelings as information: Moods influence judgments and processing strategies. In T. Gilovich, D. Griffin, & D. Kahneman (Eds.), *Heuristics and biases: The psychology of intuitive judgment* (pp. 534–547). New York: Cambridge University Press.

Schwarz, N., & Vaughn, L. A. (2002). The availability heuristic revisited: Ease of recall and content of recall as distinct sources of information. In T. Gilovich, D. Griffin, & D. Kahneman (Eds.), *Heuristics and biases: The psychology of intuitive judgment* (pp. 103–119). New York: Cambridge University Press.

Sherman, S. J., Cialdini, R. B., Schwartzman, D. F., & Reynolds, K. D. (1985). Imagination can heighten or lower the perceived likelihood of contracting a disease: The mediating effect of ease of imagery. *Personality and Social Psychology Bulletin, 11*(1), 118–127.

Slack, K., Morris, J., van Houweling, D., & Wishbow, N. (1984). Computing at Carnegie Mellon University. *Proceedings of the ACM 12th Annual Computer Science Conference on SIGCSE Symposium* (pp. 51–58). Philadelphia, PA: Association for Computing Machinery.

Sloman, S. A. (2002). Two systems of reasoning. In T. Gilovich, D. Griffin, & D. Kahneman (Eds.), *Heuristics and biases: The psychology of intuitive judgment* (pp. 379–396). New York: Cambridge University Press.

Slovic, P., Finucane, M., Peters, E., & MacGregor, D. G. (2002). The affect heuristic. In T. Gilovich, D. Griffin, & D. Kahneman (Eds.), *Heuristics and biases: The psychology of intuitive judgment* (pp. 397–420). New York: Cambridge University Press.

Tversky, A., & Kahneman, D. (1973). Availability: A heuristic for judging frequency and probability. *Cognitive Psychology, 5*, 207–232.

Tversky, A., & Kahneman, D. (1974). Judgment under uncertainty: Heuristics and biases. *Science, 185*, 1124–1131.

Tversky, A., & Kahneman, D. (1983). Extensional versus intuitive reasoning: The conjunction fallacy in probability judgment. *Psychological Review, 90*(4), 293–315.

Wiley, D. A. (2000). Connecting learning objects to instructional design theory: A definition, a metaphor, and a taxonomy. In D. A. Wiley (Ed.), *The instructional use of learning objects: Online.* Retrieved June 12, 2008, from http://reusability.org/read/chapters/wiley.doc

Wilson, T. D., & Brekke, N. (1994). Mental contamination and mental correction: Unwanted influences on judgments and evaluations. *Psychological Bulletin, 116*(1), 117–142.

Wilner, A., & Lee, J. (2002). The promise and reality of distance education. *National Education Association Update, 8*(3), 1–4.

Wilson, T. D., Centerbar, D. B., & Brekke, N. (2002). Mental contamination and the debiasing problem. In T. Gilovich, D. Griffin, & D. Kahneman (Eds.), *Heuristics and biases: The psychology of intuitive judgment* (pp. 185–200). New York: Cambridge University Press.

Wong, K. F. E., & Kwong, J. Y. Y. (2007). The role of anticipated regret in escalation of commitment. *Journal of Applied Psychology, 92*, 545–554.

Wong, K. F. E., Yik, M., & Kwong, J. Y. Y. (2006). Understanding the emotional aspects of escalation of commitment: The role of negative affect. *Journal of Applied Psychology, 91*, 282–297.

Tracey L. Leacock
Simon Fraser University
Canada

TONY DI PETTA, VERA WOLOSHYN, & JOHN. M. NOVAK

9. TOUCHING THE INTERFACE OF TECHNOLOGY

Invitational Learning with ICT

> You can never change things by fighting the existing reality. To change something, build a
> new model that makes the existing model obsolete.
>
> *Buckminister Fuller*

The use of information and communication technology (ICT) as a learning and instructional tool has become commonplace in most postsecondary institutes across North America (DiPetta, Novak, & Marini, 2003; Richards, 2005). So-called "smart-classrooms" equipped with "e-technologies" including wireless internet access, electronic projection and display systems, laptops, and hand-held computers are increasingly being used as a means for instructors and students to create new and personalized understandings of traditional content areas. Students and their instructors use these technologies to participate in on-line simulations and interact with others within the classroom or around the globe.

Although not as prevalent as in postsecondary institutions, elementary schools are beginning to incorporate ICT or e-technologies as part of their instructional repertoires, with a majority of public elementary schools having some form of access to networked information, communications technologies, and the Internet (Corbett & Willms, 2002; Smerdon, et al., 2000). At the same time, most school teachers and teacher-candidates feel largely unprepared for working with these technologies and teaching in technology-rich environments (Kirkwood, 2002; StatsCan Reports, 2007; U.S. Department of Education, 1999).

The use of ICT or e-technologies to deliver, support, or supplement classroom instruction from elementary school to higher education holds enormous implications for teachers and teacher education. The use of such technology therefore, needs to be examined prudently in order to address both the zealous enthusiasm of those smitten by the technology's capabilities and the anxiety of those fearful of its potential for intrusion into their personal and professional lives. In this chapter we discuss orientations and attitudes of teacher-candidates to the use of e-technologies as presented in their teacher-preparation program, filtered through the lens of Invitational Education (Di Petta, Novak, & Marini, 2003; Novak, 2002; Novak & Purkey, 2001) in order to establish a prudent framework for teachers and others interested in working with ICT in a democratically oriented, pedagogically derived and person-centred manner.

INVITATIONAL EDUCATION

Invitational Education is most often defined as a theory of practice that provides a framework for addressing, evaluating, and transforming the total school

T. Di Petta (Ed.), The Emperor's New Computer: ICT, Teachers and Teaching, 125–142.

environment (Novak, Rocca, & DiBiasi, 2006). It is founded on the democratic ethos, perceptual tradition and self-concept theory and is comprised of five assumptions about the nature of people and their potential for personal and professional development (Novak, 2002; Novak & Purkey, 2001; Purkey & Novak, 2008). The five assumptions are first, that people are valuable, able, and responsible and should be treated accordingly. This assumption is a commitment to the idea that all people matter, that they can grow and develop, and that they can make meaningful choices; second, that education is or should be a collaborative and cooperative activity. Implied here is the idea that educating is a "doing-with" as opposed to a "doing-to" process; third, that the process is the product in the making, an acknowledgement that how you go about doing something influences what you end up with; fourth, that people possess untapped potential in all areas of activity; and fifth, that human potential is optimized through people who invite themselves and others through intentionally planning for and designing, places, policies, programs, and processes that promote personal and professional growth (Novak & Purkey, 2001; Purkey & Novak, 1996, 2008). Applied to online environments and the use of ICT for teaching and learning, Invitational Education promotes a thoughtful and prudent approach to the planning for, and design and evaluation of, democratic virtual spaces and interactions that promote communication and development (Di Petta, Novak, & Marini, 2003).

ICT: INVITING EDUCATION AND DEMOCRATIC HOPE

The use of ICT as an educational vehicle for moving people along a personal and professional continuum of a democratic society is fundamentally an imaginative act of hope that re-envisions technology as a force for fostering positive inter-personal communication and action (Novak, & Marini, 2003; Purkey & Novak, 1996) based on John Dewey's (1916) concept of democratic structures inviting many and varied forms of communication within and between unique members of different groups. The prudent use of information and communication technologies is based on a humanistic commitment to the development of individual potential and societal practices that envisions online or technologically mediated educational environments as "enabling technologies" that assist individuals in savoring, understanding, and bettering their personal and collective experiences (Novak, 2002). The use of ICT for teaching and learning needs to be grounded in hope if it is to be positioned as an ethical and political "re-creational vehicle" for educational growth and development. Our hope in this chapter is that students and teachers not only will become competent or adept at working with ICT but that they will develop the skills and awareness needed to critically examine the underlying assumptions and consequences of working with ICT within and beyond the classroom.

A commitment to technology in education is not value-neutral. Such a commitment involves an investment of time, effort, money, and the reallocation of other scare resources into the development of a technologically-mediated education system that is based on instantaneous communication and information gratification that at present at least, privileges certain technological, economic, social, and personal interests. Education based on a democratic ethos requires its participants to examine these interests in terms of implications for democratic living and the development of a democratic society. Educators must go beyond merely technical and psychological rationales to justify the expanding influence of technology in the education community. The larger social implications of our increasing interconnection with ICT and e-technologies also need to be considered. In this chapter we model this process of inviting democratic reflection on technology's role in education by focusing our discussion and analysis on the e-classroom comparison study presented below.

THE E-CLASSROOM STUDY: CONTEXT AND RATIONALE

The technology classroom study presented here examined the beliefs and attitudes of a group of elementary-level teacher-candidates about the role of ICT or e-technology in relation to their teacher preparation program and their instructional practices as classroom teachers. All participants had been assigned to complete a required course in educational psychology in a "technology-enriched" classroom where information and communication technologies were used routinely as part of instruction. Throughout the duration of the study, data was gathered on participants' beliefs about the role of ICT as a tool for instruction and learning. The participants' experiences working with ICT and e-technologies in their practicum classrooms were also monitored.

At the time of this study, a group of 15 teacher-candidates was assigned to complete an educational psychology course in an ICT-enriched classroom where they had opportunities to download lecture materials, participate in on-line simulations, work in on-line groups, and use interactive technologies and tools to communicate with each other and the course instructor. This experience differed from that provided to a similar group of teacher-candidates assigned to a less technology oriented traditional classroom where instructional techniques included formal note taking, instructor-led demonstrations, pen-and-paper assignments, and whole-class and small-group discussions. All participants completed a demographic survey. Data revealed that all participants owned a home computer and used it extensively to complete their academic activities. At the start of the study the majority of candidates (80%) indicated that they possessed "moderate" comfort levels with respect to using information and communication technologies and credited this comfort level to their personal experiences.

Six participants from each group volunteered to participate in a series of in-depth open-ended interviews at the beginning and end of the course, as well as, following the completion of the first teaching practicum. All interviewee's were female and ranged from 23 years to 27 years of age. As part of these interviews, participants were asked to elaborate on their experiences with technology, their beliefs about how classroom teachers could use technology to support or enhance student learning, and their intentions towards using technology in their professional careers. Interviews followed standard research procedures and survey and interview data were analyzed through coding and categorizing as described by Creswell (2008), with coded data reviewed for recurring themes.

Beyond general attitudes and beliefs about the nature and role of technology in education three overarching themes emerged. These three focal points for discussion were (a) non-specific concerns or anxieties about working with technology, (b) a sense of disillusionment around the "real" or in-practice uses of technology in school classrooms, and (c) specifically career-related concerns associated with the professional responsibilities and additional duties perceived to be a function of working with e-technologies in the classroom. Examining the themes garnered from the e-classroom comparison study through the lens of Invitational Education informs a discussion of what a prudent model or approach to technology use in schools and teacher preparation programs can or should be.

A PRUDENT PERSPECTIVE DISCUSSION

A prudent approach to teaching and learning with technology requires that teachers, students, and administrators or educational policy-makers be mindful of issues and concerns that go beyond the technophile's infatuation with all things technological and the technophobe's dread of all things electronic. Invitational Education lies at the heart of the prudent approach to education with technology outlined here and it requires administrators, teachers, and learners to be *intentional, informed, inviting, integrated* and *imaginative* in their planning for and work with ICT. Discussion of the e-classroom study below is filtered through various Invitational Education lenses in order to establish a prudent framework for thinking about and planning for technology that school communities can use.

When asked to reflect on their own elementary school experiences, all teacher-candidates involved in the e-technology study indicated that they had minimal educational experiences with technology in Grades 1-8. Their recollections of technology in the classroom were limited largely to computer game playing and watching videos. Some participants recalled that there were very few computers available for student use and the ones that were available were either located at the back of the classroom or in a central location such as a laboratory or library. One participant recalled that part of her enrichment program included travelling to the school board to use their computers. In these circumstances enrichment translated into limited or restricted access that involved out-of-school planning and preparation. Many students received the message that only a few are worthy of working with technology and that only they will be able to understand or use it. Not surprising, many students subsequently feel excluded or disinvited and develop a negative attitude for learning based on the view that they "cannot do technology."

Participants agreed that opportunities to use technology were greater in secondary school, albeit still restricted to word processing, power point presentations, and limited use of the Internet. They qualified that using technology was not essential for their academic success at this level and that many of their peers elected not to use technology or take technology-related courses.

In elementary school, technology wasn't significant. Even visual aids like overheads weren't used very much. In high school we got to use computers in some of our classes.

I don't think that technology played a huge part in my learning experience in elementary school. It would have been for movies, watching videos. High school I started to do a lot more with technology. For instance, I had a geography course where the teacher introduced us to GIS technology which is pretty cool.

In contrast to their elementary and secondary school experiences, all participants perceived technology to be central to their post-secondary educational experiences. They relied on the Internet for data gathering and used word processing. The majority of their undergraduate courses included the use of WebCT or some other electronic online forum as a virtual learning environment for academic discussion.

In university, I lived on the computer. Even now I do all my research on my own computer and I don't really use the school library. I do everything on the Internet at home. I have a laptop, I have a PDA, and I have an Internet capable cell phone – technology is a big part of my life.

At the post-secondary level I used computers and the Internet for a lot of my assignments. I took a couple of distance education courses where we used WebCT, so I became quite comfortable and familiar with submitting assignments online, using discussion boards, signing in for discussion chats, and that kind of stuff...it was all part of what university was all about I guess.

Even though most of the interview participants stated that their post-secondary use of ICT was appropriate to their studies a few expressed concern about how technology was used citing experiences where course content or learning was obscured by the use of technology.

One professor used too many bells and whistles this distracted from the content of the information presented...another professor relied too much on the technology resources to supplement her own limited knowledge of content.

A prudent approach to technology use in the classroom would stress that instructional emphasis should be placed on the technology enhancing student learning. It is clear that excessive use of and reliance on technology in a lesson can be distracting and impedes student focus or learning. In order for technology to enhance student learning, instructors must engage in intentional, informed, and imaginative instructional planning. Using technology to invite teaching and learning requires the development of instructional activities that support working with technology in authentic or meaningful ways.

Another theme mined from the data collected for the e-classroom comparison study was participants' unfocused or ill-defined attitudes towards the use of technology in elementary classrooms. All participants believed that students currently enrolled in elementary and secondary schools need to possess greater technology knowledge and skills than was required for themselves. When asked about how technology should or could be integrated into their classrooms however, participants tended to provide rudimentary and limited recommendations for both teacher and student use. For example, one participant suggested that keyboarding should be taught as typing had been taught in the past. She attributed her own awareness of computer technology and her confidence in being able to learn about technology and use specific software programs to her father's insistence that the family learn to keyboard and work with software programs while she was in elementary school. Another participant suggested that using assistive technologies would be beneficial for students with learning disabilities and other exceptionalities, but did not believe that such technology should be used for basic instruction in reading and writing for all students.

> *Software that reads what's on a page to students is a real help to those students with exceptionalities who wouldn't be able to read the material in any other way... but does not help regular students develop their reading skills*

These participants' views represent technology as a specialized tool that separates "regular" from "other" students – a view that limits who and how technology can help. Such an interpretation or vision of technology in education is somewhat simplistic given current understandings of how technology can or should be used for teaching and learning. A growing body of literature suggests that assistive technology can be and is of value for all learners in schools (Thomson, Burhgstaler, & Stewart, 2003; Werger, 1998; Wood, 2001) and that e-technology needs to be unrestricted (Mistreet, Lane, & Ruffino, 2005; Parette & Stoner, 2008; Reimer-Reiss & Wacker, 1999). For many teachers, technology is used as a way of capturing students' interests and motivations for learning. In order for this invitation to learning to be meaningful and successful, teachers must invite students to use technology as a tool for research and refinement, as well as a means for presenting and sharing information in new and meaningful ways.

Another theme that emerged from the participant data was a concern about the effort required to work with technology in the classroom. Participants worried that retrieving credible information from the internet was a time consuming endeavour and that not all teachers would be willing or able to find or critique information appropriately.

> *I see a lot of teachers downloading information from the Internet and using that information as the "Bible's" truth...its not that the information is wrong but sometimes it isn't clear and it shouldn't be accepted without more proof ...just like Wikipedia isn't always right.*

The participants suggested that both students and teachers needed the knowledge and skills to evaluate critically the reliability and trustworthiness of information contained on the Internet, and acknowledged that training of these skills was not a dominant part of either the school curriculum or teacher preparation programs. The practice in many teacher preparation programs for educational technology training tends to be a survey approach that shows students a little about a wide variety of technologies rather than focusing on subject specific applications of technology.

Such an approach could be viewed as unintentionally disinviting. While the intent is to offer a broad exposure to the technology available to teachers, the reality is that the general nature of information provided tends to promote learning *about* technology rather than fostering an interest in learning how to work *with* technology as a teaching tool.

Another concern of the participants was that technology could overshadow learning in the classroom.

When instructors just read information presented with PowerPoint, the notes become the lecture instead of being used as an aid or supplement to instruction.

The participants believed that technology should not be used as an alternative to knowledge acquisition. That is, technology should not be used to hide or compensate for a lack of knowledge or skill. They worried that teachers would use technology as a "focus" versus a "supplement" to instruction thereby, "letting the tail wag the dog." These concerns appeared to be exacerbated by media reports and fearful stories about the "unreliability" of technology, especially relatively newer technologies such as smart boards and LCD projectors. The participants in the study reflected the fears of many education technology neophytes that if a technology fails they would be unable or unprepared to continue with instruction.

I don't want to end up like some of the teachers I've seen "empty handed" ...having to teach a lesson that they had planned to use some Internet material with only to have the connection not work or the bulb in the LCD goes out and not knowing what to do or fiddling with it for a long time while the class just sits there doing nothing.

One participant expressed slightly different concerns including the danger that students' use of technology might jeopardize the frequency and quality of students' social interactions,

Television, video games, and now computers seem to be aimed at younger and younger children and I'm not sure about all of this... Is watching or playing games, computer games, even the educational ones, helping children learn how to get along or play with each other... or talk to each other?

A general implication that can be drawn from the participants' statements is that the five essential foci of invitational education, *people, places, policies, processes*, and *programs* are important in developing and integrating technology with academic programming. Only by considering all of these five factors can an appropriately inviting environment be created where teachers feel confident in their ability or willingness to work with technology and students feel safe in exploring learning with technology. If the people, places, policies, processes, and programs for technology do not support teachers in working with technology they will become disillusioned and frustrated.

After completing their first teaching practicum, participants shared their observations that many schools appeared to have insufficient infrastructure and resources, and often lacked a real commitment to working with technology. Participants' practicum experiences appeared to have a dampening effect on their general enthusiasm for working with technology. Furthermore their practicum experiences tended to reinforce vague concerns about professional risks and pressures associated with working with technology on a daily basis.

Kids love technology, its motivating and exciting for them, they see it on TV, they talk about it, and they want to use it. I'm sure that it enhances their learning but my practicum didn't really show me much of how to use computers in the classroom. I guess it depends on the school you get.

Participants commented on the lack of technology use in the schools. While all participants agreed that technology was very much a part of the majority of students' lives beyond the classroom and that it consumed a substantial portion of students' free time, they acknowledged that the reverse was the case in the classroom. They witnessed minimal use of technology in the classroom and perceived that some teachers were uncertain and uncomfortable with its use.

Teachers need to possess greater knowledge of technology if they are going to stay in charge of the classroom – need to know how computers work and how to operate them – in some computer classes it does not seem that the teacher is in charge and it seems as if some students know more than the teacher about how the technology works.

A few participants suggested that schools should focus less on training students how to work with technology in light of the rapid rate at which students acquire this knowledge outside of the classroom.

In elementary education, I don't know if training how to work with technology has to play such a great role... a lot of technology is being taught in the home.

The kids have more technology toys than I did and use them better than I would be able to ... which is somewhat intimidating.

Others participants expressed distress at what they perceived to be unproductive use of instructional time where teachers were more consumed with the maintenance of the technology than with instruction per se.

When the students in my associate teacher's Grade 2 class attended computer class, the majority of the instructional time was spent logging individual students into the system resulting in limited instructional time. Students had very little time on the computers... perhaps 15 minutes out of a 40 minute class... the teacher was running around from student to student and their use was limited to playing educational games.

There was also a perception that educators were not reinforced in their attempts to use technology. Participants commented that they received little support, encouragement, or recognition when they attempted to integrate technology into their instruction as student-teachers. They perceived their efforts to use technology were further hampered by high "administrative" demands including the completion of application forms, advanced bookings, and restricted laboratory times. Collectively, participants' resulting experience was one of disappointment with respect to the use of technology in the classroom. Participants were uninspired by the types of technology currently being used in classrooms and were less optimistic about their abilities to use technology as an instructional tool as beginning teachers.

When asked about whether there were any prerequisite conditions associated with using technology in the classroom, the participants emphasized that it was the responsibility of the individual to be familiar with the technology and related software. For many, there was also the recognition that this would not be an easy task.

It's important... I have to try to push myself to try and keep learning these things and find out what else is available.

This feeling appeared to be intensified for some participants who also expressed uncertainty about how best to acquire such expertise.

I know how important it is ... to become aware of what is out there... I know I need to use it... but it is something that I don't even know where to start.

In contrast, other participants drew confidence from their previous experiences using technology and expressed greater convictions in their abilities to prepare to teach with technology, even if they did not possess specific instructional plans for instruction in content areas.

I've always been able to learn a new software program by myself within a few days – I've done it before and it doesn't scare me but ...if I had to teach a group of students right at this moment a lesson about something using technology I know I wouldn't feel very comfortable.

Regardless, all participants including the course instructor agreed that this responsibility was a time consuming one that, largely, would not be recognized by either school or university administrators.

You're not getting extra credit for it [teaching with technology]. You are not getting any recognition in terms of your professional growth, tenure or promotion. Why teach with technology? I like to do it and find it interesting. Would I advise people to be teaching with technology? Not unless they like extra work. (Instructor)

The findings of the e-classroom study suggest that these teacher- candidates benefited from participating in non-technology content courses situated in technology-enriched classrooms. Participating in such classrooms can serve to heighten teacher-candidates' appreciation and understanding of how technology can be used to enhance student learning as well as desensitize them to the challenges associated with using this instructional technology in elementary classrooms. Bai and Ertmer (2008) documented that teacher-candidates' attitudes towards technology and their views about the educational benefits associated with using technology in the classroom became more positive after completing an introductory educational technology course. However, even if such courses are used as a means of providing teacher candidates with technological awareness and experiences, teacher educators cannot assume that these future teachers will use the technology in their classrooms or use it in pedagogically effective ways (Mehlinger & Powers, 2002). Bai and Ertmer and others (Haldane, 2003; Mehlinger & Powers; Moursand & Bielefeldt, 1999; Vannatta & Beyerbach, 2000) have also demonstrated that having information and communication technologies available in schools where teacher candidates complete their field experience does not ensure its use, especially if mentor teachers or practicum supervisors do not model its use or advise teacher-candidates about how to work with these technologies.

Li (2007) documented that while practicing teachers' attitude towards technology use in schools tends to be negative, teacher-candidates' and students' attitudes towards these technologies tends to be more positive. Lam (2000) examined the reasons why some teachers avoid the use of technology in their classrooms and suggested that the perceived technophobia of teachers can often be associated with their personal beliefs about the benefits or dangers associated with technology. Lam also observed that most of these teachers had little or no experience working with technology in their classrooms so their fears were largely based on belief or ideology rather than any real fear or experiential reaction to technology.

Invitational Education stresses that the verbal, nonverbal, formal, and informal "messages" students receive every day in schools from people, places, policies, processes, and programs shape their attitudes and images about who they are and what they can do. In the same vein, the messages that schools send to teachers and teacher candidates about technology also shape teachers' attitudes and self images.

Researchers have argued that the willingness of teachers and teacher candidates to use e-classroom technologies is dependent on their experiences as recipients of these technologies (Woodbridge, 2004), their pedagogical beliefs and perceptions about their value (Darling-Hammond, 2000; Li, 2007), and their teacher education and ongoing professional development experiences (Van Braak, 2001). Until teacher education programs, policies, and practices address and re-model the use of technology in the classroom, the onus will remain with individual teachers to champion its use in the classroom. This is an unimaginative, limited, and imprudent strategy for promoting the use of technology across the curriculum or throughout a school system. What is required is a framework for working collaboratively and intentionally on planning for the prudent implementation and use of technology in schools.

A FRAMEWORK FOR ICT PLANNING: THE PRUDENT EDUCATIONAL TECHNOLOGY CHECKLIST

Integrating technology into schools and education programs in a prudent and inviting manner requires administrators and educators to base their planning and classroom interactions with and about technology on the Invitational Education premise that everything and everybody adds to or subtracts from connecting with students in meaningful ways (Purkey & Novak, 2008). Ideally, technological environments in schools should be intentionally designed and maintained so that people, places, policies, programs, and processes are focused on and working to support a democratic environment where every individual member of the school community is invited to develop the full range of his or her intellectual, technical, expressive, and social abilities. Being both inviting and prudent about the use of technology in our schools and classrooms means looking at how technology can be integrated into an educative environment in terms of the people, places, policies, programs, and processes that shape and share that environment. The following checklist can be used as part of an assessment and planning activity by members of a school community, administrators, teachers, staff, students, and parents to intentionally integrate people and technology in an environment that informs people of their positive worth, ability, and self-efficacy. Completing the checklist and totalling the results for each of the categories provides the basis for discussing how to create a technologically supported democratic learning environment based on imaginative acts of hope and trust in the human-technology interface.

People	*Strongly disagree*	*Disagree*	*Neither disagree nor agree*	*Agree*	*Strongly agree*
	1	2	3	4	5
Teachers, administrators, students, parents, and staff are informed about an involved in discussion on how information and communication technology (ICT) is used at this school.					
Administrators encourage faculty and staff with professional development in ICT..					
Teachers support and encourage all students in using ICT.					
Teachers provide all students with opportunities to work with ICT.					
Parents feel their ICT opinions and concerns are considered and dealt with fairly by teachers and administrators.					

The Prudent Educational Technology Checklist

Please mark your response to each of the statements by circling the appropriate number, with 1 for strongly disagree to 5 for strongly agree. Please keep in mind that these ratings are meant to be viewed as a starting point for school-community or planning team discussions about how technology can and should be used in a democratic educational system. Use this checklist to celebrate achievements and reflect on new possibilities for prudently integrating technology into educational environments.

Places	Strongly disagree	Disagree	Neither disagree nor agree	Agree	Strongly agree
	1	2	3	4	5
Technology adds to and fits in well with the clean, well-maintained, and attractive appearance of this school.					
Networked computers are available in labs, the library, classrooms, and student work areas.					
Virtual work and communication spaces on school-based learning or conferencing systems are kept updated and provide relevant information for teachers, students, and parents					
Work areas are well-lit, uncluttered, accessible to all, and conveniently located.					
The school's web pages present ICT policies and information in clear, accurate, and jargon free language.					

Policies	Strongly disagree	Disagree	Neither disagree nor agree	Agree	Strongly agree
	1	2	3	4	5
Teachers, students, parents, and administrators are involved in the policy development process for ICT.					
Acceptable use policies and general rules for ICT are clear, well-posted, and fairly administered.					
It is a policy that teachers are updated, supported, and recognized for working with technology.					
School policy encourages teachers and non-teaching staff to use technology for professional development and personal growth.					
Policies link ICT with the attainment of specific and explicit academic goals.					

Programs	Strongly disagree	Disagree	Neither disagree nor agree	Agree	Strongly agree
	1	2	3	4	5
Technology programs involve out-of-school experiences that link to the community and the world.					
School programs encourage teachers and students to explore technology, its uses, and meaning for society.					
Programs allow students a reasonable say in determining their technology activities.					
Programs are planned with student interests, life and career goals, and technology skills in mind.					
Programs are flexible and support student access to learning through a variety of ways including but not limited to the use of information and communication technologies.					

Processes	Strongly disagree	Disagree	Neither disagree nor agree	Agree	Strongly agree
	1	2	3	4	5
Parents receive a response to an e-mail or phone request within a reasonable length of time.					
Administrators and teachers routinely use ICT to communicate with parents, students, and the greater school community.					
Teachers maintain and explain clear and reasonable technology goals and assignments, keeping in mind student learning styles and interests.					
Teachers are available for students through online or other ICT means but also in person before and after school.					
All students have the right and feel welcome to use ICT when and if they need to.					

Source: All tables adapted from Di Petta, Novak, & Marini (2003)

CONCLUSION

From an invitational perspective, teaching with and about technology needs to be an integral component of both teacher education programs and school communities if it is going to enable all students to grasp its educational potential. It should not be restricted to "special" occasions nor presented in a "what I say" rather than "what I do" fashion (Bai & Ertmer, 2008). Unfortunately, the findings of the study presented here suggest that the reality of teacher education programs and many schools may be far removed from this ideal. Beyond the use of power point presentations, participants reported limited experiences involving the integration of technology into their classes. Without such integration and modeling, invitations to working with technology are seen as empty and are thus often declined. The findings of the e-class study also challenge teacher educators to consider how best to integrate technology as an instructional tool, especially with respect to balancing the illusion of "technological transparency" in which using the technology is made to look simpler or easier than it really is. Promoting the use of technology as an "instructional tool" means modeling the problem solving skills required to address technological difficulties and/or failures during the instructional process. Moreover, teacher educators need to be mindful that while they are preparing teacher-candidates to teach in the classrooms of today they also need to provide them with the knowledge and skills necessary for teaching in the "technologically enriched" classrooms of tomorrow.

Many teachers complain that they cannot savor, understand, or better their experiences with technology because they feel rushed, overloaded with information, and not able to reflect meaningfully on what they are doing or why. Many like the participants in the e-classroom comparison study subscribe to a set of media and technology industry driven myths about what technology can do for education and the benefits of using it in the classroom. The claims of what e-technology can do for teachers and learners are often unrealistic or untested in real-world settings and based on the overarching myth that maintains that "technology is the answer." This implies that everyone agrees on what the question is. This myth has implicitly become a mantra in education systems worldwide and it assumes that there is common agreement on the what, how, and why of technology's use in schools and more generally in education. However, when it comes to technology in education it is clear that one size does not fit all. A prudent approach is called for to address the anxieties of technophobes and the hopes of technophiles and ensure the pedagogical effectiveness of e-technologies in our schools.

Working with technologies in the classroom will succeed in promoting a democratic educative environment to the extent that teachers are able to use the technology in a framework that supports and preserves dignity and encourages communication between and among individuals and groups working towards an educative goal. Alternatively, if teachers use the information and communication technologies to overload students with information or inundate them with "busy work" rather than meaningful learning opportunities then students react like deer caught in the headlights of an oncoming vehicle, frozen in their tracks and unable to move in any direction. The aim of this chapter was to present a prudent approach to thinking about and planning for the use of ICT or e-technologies in school environments and to invite readers to touch the human face of technology in education because it will always be the human touch that ensures that technology is a vehicle for educational growth and development.

REFERENCES

Bai, H., & Ertmer, P. (2008). Teacher-educators' beliefs and technology uses as predictors of preservice teachers' beliefs and technology attitudes. *Journal of Technology and Teacher Education, 16*(1), 93–112.

Corbett, B., & Willms, J. D. (2002). *Canadian students' access to and use of information and communication technology.* Retrieved May 1, 2008, from http://www.cesc-csce.ca/pceradocs/2002/papers/BCorbett_OEN.pdf

Creswell, J. W. (2008). *Educational research: Planning, conducting, and evaluating quantitative and qualitative research.* Upper Saddle River, NJ: Merrill Prentice Hall.

Darling-Hammond, L. (2000). Teacher quality and student achievement: A review of state policy evidence. *Education Policy Analysis Archives, 8*(1). Retrieved May 1, 2008, from http://olam.ed.asu.edu/epaa/v8n1/

Dewey, J. (1916). *Democracy and education.* New York., The Macmillan Company.

DiPetta, T., Novak, J., & Marini, Z. (2003). *Inviting online education.* Phi Delta Kappan Fastback. Bloomington, IL: Phi Delta Kappa Educational Foundation.

Haldane, M. (2003). *Real-time lesson observation: Using technology in teacher training to learn about technology in the classroom.* Retrieved January 1, 2008, from http://www.celt.mmu.ac.uk/ltia/issue6/haldane.shtml

Kirkwood, J. J. (2002). The status of technology education in elementary schools as reported by beginning teachers. *Journal of Industrial Teacher Education, 37*(3), 93–114.

Lam, Y. (2000). Technophilia vs. technophobia: A preliminary look at why second-language teachers do or do not use technology in their classrooms. *Canadian Modern Languages Review, 56*(3), 389–420.

Li, Q. (2007). Student and teacher views about technology: A tale of two cities? *Journal of Research on Technology in Education, 39*(4), 377–397.

Mehlinger, H. D., & Powers, S. M. (2002). *Technology and teacher education: A guide for educators and policymakers.* Boston, MA: Houghton Mifflin.

Mistreet, S. G., Lane, S. J., & Ruffino, A. G. (2005). Growing and learning through technology: Birth to five. In D. Edyburn, K. Higgins, & R. Boone (Eds.), *Handbook of special education technology research and practice* (pp. 273–307). Whitefish Bay, WI: Knowledge by Design.

Moursund, D., & Bielefeldt, T. (1999). *Will new teachers be prepared to teach in a digital age? A national survey on information technology in teacher education.* Milken Family Foundation. Retrieved June 14, 2008, from http://www.mff.org/pubs/ME154.pdf

Novak, J. M. (2002). *Inviting educational leadership: Fulfilling potential and applying an ethical perspective to the educational process.* London: Pearson.

Novak, J. M., & Purkey, W. W. (2001). *Invitational education.* Bloomington, IN: Phi Delta Kappa.

Novak, J. M., Rocca, W., & DiBiasi, A. M. (2006). *Creating inviting schools.* San Francisco, CA: Caddo Gap Press.

Parette, H. P., & Stoner, J. B. (2008). Benefits of assistive technology user groups for early childhood education professional. *Early Childhood Education Journal, 35*(4), 301–389.

Purkey, W. W., & Novak, J. M. (1996). *Inviting school success: A self-concept approach to teaching, learning, and democratic practice* (3rd ed.). Belmont, CA: Wadsworth.

Purkey, W. W., & Novak, J. M. (2008). *Fundamentals of invitational education.* Atlanta, GA: International Alliance for Invitational Education.

Richards, C. (2005). The design of effective ICT-supported learning activities: Exemplary models, changing requirements, and new possibilities. *Language Learning and Technology, 9*(1), 60–79. Retrieved May 1, 2008, from http://llt.msu.edu/vol9num1/pdf/richards.pdf

Reimer-Riess, M. L., & Wacker, R. R. (1999). Assistive technology use and abandonment among college students with disabilities. *International Electronic Journal for Leadership in Learning, 3*(23). Retrieved April 21, 2008, from http://www.ucalgary.ca/~iejll

Smerdon, B., Cronen, S., Lanahan, L., Anderson, J., Iannotti, N., & Angeles, J., et al. (2000). *Teacher's tools for the 21st Century: A report on teachers' use of technology* (NCES 2000-102). Washington, DC: United States Department of Education, National Center for Education Statistics.

StatsCan Reports. (2007). *Connectivity and ICT integration in Canadian elementary and secondary schools: First results from the information and communications technologies in schools survey,* 2003/04, 17, 81-595-MIE2004017. Retrieved May 1, 2008, http://www.statcan.ca/Daily/English/040610/d040610b.htm

Thompson, T., Burgstahler, S., & Stewart, R. (2003). Beyond web accessibility: Technology accessibility policies in higher education. *Proceedings from the Center of Disabilities Technology and Persons with Disabilities Conference,.* Northridge, CA. Retrieved April 19, 2008, from http://www.csun.edu/cod/conf/2003/proceedings/172.htm

U.S. Department of Education (1999). *NCES teacher quality: A report on the preparation and qualifications of public school teachers.* Retrieved January 1, 2008, from http:www.PT3.org

Van Braak, J. (2001). Individual characteristics influencing teachers' class use of computers. *Journal of Educational Computing Research, 25*(2), 141–157.

Vannatta, R. A., & Beyerbach, B. (2000). Facilitating a constructivist vision of technology integration among education faculty and pre-service teachers. *Journal of Research on Computing in Education, 33*(2), 132–148.

Werger, C. (1998). *Integrating assistive technology into the standard curriculum.* Reston, VA: ERIC Clearinghouse on Disabilities and Gifted Education. (ERIC Document Reproduction Services No. ED426517)

Woodbridge, J. (2004). Technology integration as a transforming teaching strategy. *Technology and Learning Magazine.* Retrieved May 1, 2008, from http://techlearning.com/showArticle.jhtml?Article ID=17701367

Wood, J. M. (2001, April). Every kid can! *Instructor.* Retrieved April 18, 2008 from http://findarticles.com/cf_0/m0STR/2001_April/73088568/print.jhtml

Tony Di Petta
Brock University
Canada

Vera Woloshyn
Brock University
Canada

John M. Novak
Brock University
Canada

Lightning Source UK Ltd.
Milton Keynes UK
171433UK00001B/7/P